"*The Voices of Nationals: Why Training the Indigenous Works to Move and Multiply the Gospel* by Dr. Bruce Snavely is a groundbreaking and timely contribution to the global missions conversation. With clarity, conviction, and compassion, Snavely challenges long-held assumptions about Western missionary models and offers a biblically faithful, historically proven, and practically effective alternative: empowering indigenous leaders through theological training. Drawing from over a decade of firsthand experience across Africa and beyond, this book is not just theory—it is testimony. Through powerful stories of national pastors transformed by training and now transforming their nations, Snavely demonstrates that the future of missions lies in the hands of those who already live, speak, and serve among the people they are called to reach. This book is a must-read for pastors, mission boards, seminary leaders, and anyone passionate about fulfilling the Great Commission. It will inspire, challenge, and equip you to rethink your role in global missions and to invest where the return is eternal. I wholeheartedly recommend *The Voices of Nationals* as a vital resource for the twenty-first-century church. It is not only a book—it is a catalyst for the biblical fulfillment of the Great Commission."

—MIKE GRIFFIN, Missions Director, First Baptist Melbourne, Florida

"The command of the Lord to 'go' seems so simple and yet so involved. In this helpful volume, Dr. Snavely guides readers to consider the topic of missions but reconsider how to accomplish it. The practical wisdom paired with first-hand accounts calls Christians and churches to step into a wonderful—though maybe unfamiliar—way of doing the Great Commission like never before."

—PAUL NORTON, Senior Pastor, Faith Baptist Church, Dayton, Ohio

"*The Voices of Nationals* is an insightful explanation of the pastoral and missionary training model of the Global Baptist Training Foundation which follows the well-known instruction of the Apostle Paul to Timothy found in 2 Timothy 2:1–7. In this short but captivating book, Dr. Snavely lays out the 'Why,' 'What,' and 'How' of the GBTF modular training program that God has used to impact the lives and ministries of thousands of national, indigenous pastors, church planters, and believers over the last thirteen years across multiple African countries in the 10/40 window. Not only does 'Dr. Bruce' detail the strategy of the GBTF program to successfully bring biblically sound theological and practical instruction to nationals where they are, but he also includes the priceless and amazing testimonies of key indigenous pastors and church leaders whose lives and ministries have been powerfully impacted and changed through the GBTF training. For anyone wanting insights into a 'nationals training nationals' missionary ministry program that God is greatly blessing and using for the cause of the gospel and his glory, I can heartily recommend this book."

—JOHN MOORE, served in pastoral ministry for twenty years in Michigan and Wisconsin

"Through vivid stories and clarifying insights, Dr. Snavely effectively illustrates the transformative power of providing consistent and practical theological training to local pastors across the globe. *Voices of the Nationals* presents a vision for sustainable missionary efforts and serves as a testament to the resilience and faith of indigenous church leaders. The Global Baptist Training Foundation is proving to be a 'pace setter' for organizations that aspire to be truly gospel-centered and mission-minded."

—SPENCER MARTIN, Missions and College Pastor, Two Cities Church, Winston-Salem, North Carolina

"I have had the privilege of working with Bruce Snavely in training nationals in Liberia, Uganda, Rwanda, and Tanzania over a three-or-four-year period. It was an amazing learning experience for me to see how practical and biblically based this method of equipping national pastors was. I have worked with two other organizations through the years that did similar work. However, GBTF has been the most effective in their strategy of equipping the pastors to multiply by becoming trainers themselves. After working a few years in the countries I mentioned above, I had worked myself out of a job! The nationals multiplied our work to reach other nationals more effectively than I could once they learned the materials. This book, *The Voices of the Nationals*, is a very readable layout of the strategy used to reach all of Africa with nationals training and equipping nationals. It is exciting to read what God has done through GBTF over these past twelve years. It is even more exciting what God will continue to do as we experience the multiplication of trainers developing more trainers."

—LARRY BAZER, Pastor Emeritus, First Baptist Church, Melbourne, Florida

"As a pastor who has wrestled with how our church can most effectively advance the Great Commission, I find *The Voices of the Nationals* presents a compelling case for rethinking traditional missions strategy. Dr. Snavely's thirteen-year experience with Global Baptist Training Foundation offers concrete evidence that training indigenous leaders produces exponentially greater results than our typical Western missionary model. The book's strength lies in letting national pastors speak for themselves about what they actually need and want: theological training, not dependency. The biblical foundation in 2 Timothy 2:1–7 is solid, and the multiplication principle is clearly apostolic. The financial arguments alone should make every missions committee take notice. The core principle is undeniable: nationals reaching nationals with proper theological training works. Every church serious about global impact should grapple with these ideas. This book challenges us to move beyond supporting missionaries to empowering movements. I recommend this for pastors, missions committees, and anyone involved in global ministry strategy. It may not change everything you do, but it will certainly change how you think about what you do."

—MIKE WOODWARD, Lead Pastor, Church of the Cross, Smithfield, Rhode Island

"In *Voices of the Nationals*, Dr. Bruce Snavely challenges the traditional foreign mission model, not to criticize but to awaken the church to the remarkable fruitfulness God is producing through national pastors around the world. With compelling firsthand stories and irrefutable data, this book shows how empowering and training nationals is not only biblical (2 Tim. 2:1–7), it's essential to obeying the Great Commission. Through the work of the Global Baptist Training Foundation, over 1,500 churches have been planted in the past decade, tens of thousands of souls have come to Christ, and thousands more have followed in baptism. This movement is growing exponentially not so much by 'strategic partnerships' but by national ownership. Dr. Snavely reveals a model where American resources serve, not lead, the gospel advance. Be prepared to be encouraged, challenged, and yes, even uncomfortable. The voices of trained national leaders echo throughout these pages, declaring with clarity and conviction that the harvest is ready. The baton is being passed and it's multiplying exponentially. If we truly want to reach the nations, we must trust, train, and release those already called from among the nations. This book captures the biblical blueprint that is producing unprecedented spiritual fruit for the glory of God."

—DERIC BARTLETT, Senior Pastor, City Centre Church, Mississauga, Ontario, Canada

# The Voices of Nationals

# The Voices of Nationals

Why Training the Indigenous Moves
and Multiplies the Gospel Forward

BRUCE SNAVELY

*Prologue by Fidele Shinga*
*Foreword by Scott Wilson*

WIPF & STOCK · Eugene, Oregon

THE VOICES OF NATIONALS
Why Training the Indigenous Moves and Multiplies the Gospel Forward

Copyright © 2025 Bruce Snavely. All rights reserved. Except for brief quotations in critical publications or reviews, no part of this book may be reproduced in any manner without prior written permission from the publisher. Write: Permissions, Wipf and Stock Publishers, 199 W. 8th Ave., Suite 3, Eugene, OR 97401.

Wipf & Stock
An Imprint of Wipf and Stock Publishers
199 W. 8th Ave., Suite 3
Eugene, OR 97401

www.wipfandstock.com

PAPERBACK ISBN: 979-8-3852-5988-5
HARDCOVER ISBN: 979-8-3852-5989-2
EBOOK ISBN: 979-8-3852-5990-8

11/21/25

Scripture quotations are from The ESV® Bible (The Holy Bible, English Standard Version®), © 2001 by Crossway, a publishing ministry of Good News Publishers. Used by permission. All rights reserved.

# Contents

| | | |
|---|---|---|
| *Prologue by Fidele Shinga* | | vii |
| *Foreword by Scott Wilson* | | xi |
| *Preface* | | xiii |
| *Introduction* | | xv |
| Chapter One | The Great Commission: What and How? | 1 |
| Chapter Two | What Is the Mission of Missions? | 8 |
| Chapter Three | Contemporary Missions: Two Key Questions | 32 |
| Chapter Four | Why Train the Nationals? | 50 |
| Chapter Five | What Has Happened? | 77 |
| Chapter Six | Protocols for Change | 94 |
| *Epilogue* | | 103 |
| *Conclusion* | | 105 |
| *Bibliography* | | 107 |

# Prologue

I DIDN'T KNOW HOW to breathe, what to do, where to start—not only physically, but also spiritually and emotionally. I woke up each day and felt hopeless with a deep heaviness in my heart. My life was stagnated and stuck.

In all, I trusted the Lord God, hoping that one day I would definitely come out of this situation. I had reached the end of myself. I was a believer in Jesus Christ. In fact, I was pastor of an influential Baptist church in the capitol city of Rwanda.

Life was hard. I was a married man with two daughters then, but most of the time, I was unable not only to feed my family, but also to fulfill other different responsibilities as a man in the house.

It wasn't just about physical needs. I was spiritually poor and lacked biblical knowledge. Imagine being a church pastor without any theological training. This was not only bad but also dangerous because leading without knowledge will end up misleading the people of God.

Then the light of God shined into my life.

In July 2013, God brought an organization called Global Baptist Training Foundation (GBTF) into Rwanda to train our pastors. They came to Rwanda, my country, to the city of Kigali. I started interpreting for them, driving them, picking them up from the airport to the hotel, from the hotel to the church for theological training classes. GBTF came in the middle of my panic, not knowing where my help would come.

For almost six years, I served God with them sacrificially, committed to the work of ministry without looking back.

## PROLOGUE

*Remember life was hard!* Sometimes I would walk home after parking the church vehicle because I was not allowed to drive it home. But I trusted the Lord and remained faithful to him and to my organization leaders.

Truly, God is faithful, and his faithfulness shall remain forever. Through GBTF, God changed my life. I learned more than any of the other students because, as translator, I had to grasp and understand each theological concept in order to fully pass it on to the pastors.

Like the other fifty-five pastors attending these classes in Rwanda, I was already in ministry serving without any theological training. The genocide had left us without access to theological education or the ability to pay for it if it was available. Glory be to the almighty God for sending GBTF's mobile training of this caliber to my country, particularly to the church where I was serving God with only little knowledge. GBTF came to train me, equip me for better service unto my Christ Jesus. I did not know then what the impact of this training would do

Dr. Bruce Snavely not only taught me, but he also mentored me as a father in the ministry. As my teacher, he emphasized stewardship, faithfulness, and many other core values. I am now equipped, theologically trained, and well prepared for the work of ministry, ready to teach others according to 2 Tim 2:1–7. I felt the deep burden to pass this training on to others.

Eventually, Dr. Bruce appointed me as the East Africa trainer, and I started training the men in many countries of East Africa like Rwanda, Burundi, Tanzania, Kenya, Congo, and Ethiopia. Dr. Bruce had the vision to develop the theological training materials for fourteen separate classes and to have these materials translated into the languages in each country. He also began the practice of having all class materials reproduced so that each pastor took home the class materials to do continued study as well as to use these materials to train their own church members and even other pastors.

God did great things that I may not be able to talk about except a few of them. *Hear this!* God is using me under the leadership

## PROLOGUE

of Dr. Bruce to accomplish more than I could have ever imagined! What took Dr. Bruce a decade took me less than five years. In a very short period of time, my team and I were able to reach and accomplish more. Why? Here are answers:

- Nationals training nationals
- Knowing the languages
- Understanding how to navigate the culture
- Living with and loving the people

God used all these to accelerate his work for a fraction of the cost compared to the Western missionaries who come to Africa from afar, at very high costs, without knowing the languages, culture, and how people live.

Later I started teaching beyond East Africa! I reached out to West Africa, Central Africa, and Southern Africa, teaching what I had learned and training the men to be trainers of others in the future. I have now become the Africa-wide director for the GBTF.

We now reach about twenty-eight of the African nations with our GBTF training. We have 200 national trainers who have completed the GBTF curriculum as well as specific training to be a trainer with our materials. We are starting churches through these GBTF-trained pastors faster than is imaginable—1,600 to date. Thousands of pastors are being trained; tens of thousands are coming to faith in Christ and being baptized through these church plants. Our church plants are discipling all new believers as we have learned in our GBTF training. It is difficult to imagine how God is using GBTF to change the face of the African continent. Revival is taking place across Africa. That revival was sparked by the mission of training nationals to train nationals. It is palpable.

God bless you in Jesus name. Love you so much.

FIDELE SHINGA
Africa Director, Global Baptist Training Foundation
2 Tim 2:1–7

# Foreword

WRITTEN AS A FOLLOW-UP to his previous book, *Indigenous*, Dr. Bruce Snavely has given us a wonderful gift with this latest work, *The Voices of the Nationals*.

In these pages you will find the incredible story of what God has done through Dr. Snavely's ministry, the Global Baptist Training Foundation (GBTF), and how through the training of indigenous pastors, the gospel is sweeping through large swaths of the continent of Africa with life-changing power.

This book is a gift to the church for several reasons. First, it's a gift because it holds up a model of missions that is biblically sound. I'm confident everyone reading this book believes in raising up and sending out missionaries to the nations as we seek to fulfill the Great Commission our Lord gave us (Matt 28:18–20). The church I am blessed to pastor, where Bruce and Grave Snavely and their family worship and serve, has a goal of raising up one hundred missionaries in the next ten years. The apostle Paul himself was sent out as a missionary by his local church at Antioch. But, as is made clear in this book, Paul's model of ministry was to raise up leaders in every church he planted. He trained and equipped those leaders not only to shepherd the believers in their local church, but to lead the church in taking the gospel into the surrounding areas. The ministry of GBTF on the continent of Africa, and beyond, has been in keeping with this biblical model of mission work.

Second, this book is a gift because it is a cause for the church to celebrate the great things that God has done. How do we wrap our minds around the fruitfulness of GBTF's ministry in just over

FOREWORD

a decade's time? In the last twelve years, they have seen 3,000 pastors trained, 1,500 new churches planted, and tens of thousands of new followers of Christ! We know the Spirit blows where He wishes, and the Lord is the One who builds his church, and to him be all the glory. But it is right for those who love the nations, and long to see "all the peoples praise" him (Ps 67:5), to pause and thank God for this mighty gospel movement happening right now on the African continent.

Lastly, this book is a gift because of the stories it contains. God made us to love stories and to be moved by them. Perhaps that's why about half of the Bible is given to us in narrative form. This book contains stories—lots of them. Stories of people saved, lives changed, pastors trained, churches planted, and impact multiplied. Let's read them, learn from them, and be motivated by them to pour our lives out so that all may hear of the great glory of our King Jesus.

DR. SCOTT WILSON
Lead Pastor, First Baptist Church, Melbourne, Florida

# Preface

HAVING A REAL CONVERSATION with an indigenous pastor is certainly an unusual occurrence for most people. I must admit that for forty years of ministry leading up to this current chapter of life in training national pastors, I had never sat down and talked face-to-face with any national pastors or church leaders about much of anything. I definitely had never asked them about what they thought regarding the best way to advance the gospel in their countries, or anywhere, for that matter.

Now, in our thirteenth year of training indigenous church leaders all over the globe, I have had that conversation countless times. It has been a journey of discovery, and also a journey of humility in what God has both shown us and allowed this training process to accomplish. In the next few pages you will read about not only the New Testament philosophy of missions Paul bequeathed to Timothy, but what God can do when we obey it on his terms.

In every chapter you will be introduced to various national pastors in the narrative who have some important things to say about how missions ought to look if we are going to move and multiply the gospel forward in our world. Then following each chapter where those national pastors have offered insight, their individual stories will be provided for greater context. Whatever you do, don't miss the stories! They are so entwined with the narrative that if you ignore them, you will miss more than their story. Because many of these men of God live in dangerous areas of the world, primarily on the continent of Africa, their names have not

PREFACE

been used to identify them. However, their histories identify how vital they consider their training is for ministry in being able to advance the kingdom of God where they live and most likely will also die.

May God bless each of them, and may God bless us as we ponder their words, opinions, and insights as to how we can exponentially multiply the gospel into our twenty-first-century world.

# Introduction

NEARLY FIFTEEN YEARS AGO God began a journey in my life that would lead to training indigenous church leaders globally. What we have discovered about biblical missions since that day has been truly life-changing, to say the least. A key part of this discovery is rooted in a new appreciation of what the apostle Paul taught about training and establishing local pastors in the areas where they live and minister.

Another part of this discovery was that the indigenous national pastors we have encountered told us many things that we as Westerners desperately needed to hear in our own generation. If the apostle Paul was accurate in his admonition to train, ordain, and empower elders from their own locales to lead their local assemblies, then it is a principle that we cannot permit to be omitted or ignored in our missions philosophy.

For the indigenous church leader, knowledge is truly power, and they will sacrifice deeply to access biblical training for their ministries. I have known these many men and woman to sacrifice in ways that continuously challenge my Western worldview of what it means to serve our eternal God. There is no complaining to be heard among them. They arrive at class after arduous travel and raise their calloused hands in praise to God for safety. They sleep on cement floors with a thin foam pad and a blanket, thankful they can be part of new class.

Finally, it is important to recognize the incredible potential of training indigenous pastors and church leaders. The accomplishments of these theologically trained nationals are truly staggering.

## INTRODUCTION

In the following chapters the insights and stories of what we have come to understand about national church leaders are going to be told. Because of the instability of many of their countries, their names and exact locations will not be disclosed. However, all of them fearlessly serve Jesus Christ wherever they are, whether in pastoring their own congregations, training other nationals, or launching new church plants. Our prayer is that God would bless and keep them as well as uplift you with their courage and conviction in ministry.

In this book you will be introduced to some of the toughest, most resilient individuals I have ever had the pleasure of working with in ministry. For many of them, they are blessed to simply be alive, having faced almost insurmountable odds in many of their life experiences. From genocides, civil wars, disease, and countless other near-death events, they show us that it is not what we go through that's important, but that we endure the pain and suffering in reaching a higher goal. When I get up each morning now after witnessing their lives up close for well over a decade, I breathe a prayer of thanksgiving for God's mercy in my life. Only God knows why I am allowed to live a life free from the treacheries which daily accost many of my student pastors.

In each of these brief vignettes woven into each chapter, I hope you see that they have more than their own story to tell. They are really painting the portraits of how God has prepared them to do what only they can do. The African continent is both a vast and difficult place to carve out a life. But, unlike many of us in America, they *instinctively* know that they need a community to survive. However, as spiritual leaders, they need more than that; they deeply aspire to theological training. For them, this training is the engine that drives everything else. When theologically prepared, their churches become vibrant and alive with forms of worship that are at once uniquely African but intensely Christian in their focus. They know that without biblical education and training, the gospel cannot be moved and multiplied forward over generations.

# CHAPTER ONE

## The Great Commission: What and How?

WHEN JESUS ADDRESSED THE disciples in the Galilean hill country prior to his imminent departure, he set the stage for what would become his command to the church for the ages found in Matt 28:18–20. His command answers the great question for all of Christ's church-age disciples regarding God's agenda. What Jesus said was general in scope but specific enough in detail to answer the immediate and long-term question regarding *what* the church was to do in his absence.

However, we know the church was considerably slow in its initial response to Christ's universal command to his people. In fact, in the book of Acts, it takes literally eleven chapters for the churches to break out into a universal proclamation of the gospel to both Jew and gentile. Beginning with Paul's conversion to Christ and Peter's vision in Acts 9 and 10, the call to reach the gentile world was being realized, and the first-century church began to expand into multiple churches scattered across Asia and the Macedonian world.

In spite of the Apostle to the Gentiles' success, he endured multiple challenges and imprisonments. After a two-year imprisonment in Caesarea between AD 58–60, Paul was sent to Rome and was under house arrest there for another two years, anticipating his release. He was released after writing his captivity letters to Philippi, Ephesus, Colossae, and then his personal letter to Philemon. According to Phil 1:25, the apostle was eagerly anticipating his freedom with the privilege of continued service to his beloved Philippians and others.

Upon his release it is likely Paul made his way to Spain where there are significant historical reasons for believing he had fulfilled his long-held desire to take the gospel to one of the farthest reaches of the empire between AD 62–64. We do not have a timeline involving this fourth missionary journey to Spain and the Macedonian churches to which he ministered before his terminal arrest. Perhaps after departing Spain he may have made his way to Crete to visit Titus, where he instructed him to appoint local pastor/elders in every city. He then possibly would have gone on to Ephesus to visit his beloved Timothy, followed by his visit to the other Macedonian churches in which he had lovingly ministered. It was likely at this time that he wrote Timothy the first epistle bearing his name. He would have then likely made stops in Miletus and Troas, among other cities in Macedonia such as Corinth and Nicopolis.

Finally, in the heat of Nero's persecution of Christians throughout the capitol and throughout the empire, Paul was finally rearrested and brought to Rome, where he was placed in the infamous Mamertine Prison sometime around winter in either AD 65 or 66. The darkness of this time in Paul's life cannot be underestimated. Paul was facing what he likely knew would be a brief and final season of life.

With time being short, his ministry appeared at first glance to be teetering on failure. All of his ministry associates in Asia had abandoned him and the ministry for various reasons, none of them good. He named those who had forsaken him and those who had opposed him. Fortunately, all human connection was not lost. He had Luke, the beloved apostle. Surprising to some, the apostle requested that John Mark be sent to him. This relationship, long restored, had earlier been bitterly broken over unknown reasons

## THE GREAT COMMISSION: WHAT AND HOW?

involving Mark's departure from the first missionary journey. Paul now sought for him to come visit during these final months. Then the apostle clearly tells his young pastor:

> For I am already being poured out as a drink offering, and the time of my departure has come. I have fought the good fight, I have finished the race. (2 Tim 4:6–7 ESV)

The drink offering was the final element of the Old Testament offering. Paul seems to be indicating that the offering of his life as a ministry sacrifice is nearing its completion with his being loosed or released through death to be present with the Lord he loves. It appears abundantly clear that Paul's mental state is embracing the certain reality of his ensuing passage into the glorious kingdom of his Savior Jesus Christ. In his absence from the scene, Paul had to be assured that his life investment in the gospel would not be abandoned as the ministry was by many of his present associates. Knowing all of this, the apostle lays out *how* the gospel would be moved and multiplied into an uncertain future. He had long identified Timothy as the young, careful, and teachable ministry associate upon whom he would lay the gospel mantle. In what we may define as the second phase of the Christ's initial command to the Twelve in the Gospels, Paul sets forth to Timothy in his final letter that, after evangelizing a certain area, the church would perpetuate itself by continuously training local leaders. This would be a continuous plan up through the close of the apostolic era and beyond.

Within this brief set of directions in 2 Tim 2:1–7, the apostle establishes a simple yet profound plan answering the question of *how* the gospel can be effectively and perpetually moved and multiplied into coming generations. For instance, in Acts 14:23, Paul and Barnabas "appointed elders for them in every church" in Lystra, Iconium, Derbe, and other areas of Southern Galatia. Acts 18:11 shows that Paul spent eighteen months in Corinth teaching and training and then left the local leaders in charge to continue the work (Acts 20:31). In Ephesus, Paul taught for three years and then left the local elders to lead the work forward. In Titus 1:3, on the island of Crete, Paul commanded Titus to "appoint

## Voices of the Nationals

elders in every town as I directed you." The concept being taught here both implicitly and explicitly is the principle of training and installing local leadership over local churches.

What had begun with Christ's original command in Matt 28 to the Twelve on *what* they were to do was now to continue on this basis until the end of the age. Now, thirty years later, the incomparable Apostle to the Gentiles lays out a strategy to ensure perpetual multiplication of the gospel.

These four simple concepts in 2 Tim 2:2 begin with a command:

1. Commit! ... Entrust to ...

This idea carries the idea of handing off something extremely valuable to someone else. The picture it conveys is that of entrusting a *valuable* yet *vulnerable* object to another. In other words, we are not just handing someone an everyday item when we pass the gospel baton. We are entrusting them with the most costly commodity on earth. It is the good news that shatters the darkness of our world like a lightning bolt in the midst of a dark thunderstorm. The gospel is the light which the world desperately requires to live! We have been entrusted with the message of the death, burial, and resurrection of Christ. With the gospel the world lives; without it the world perishes in sin. This word "entrust" becomes highly significant to the rest of the passage because it establishes the incredible value of what we have been entrusted with regarding the gospel of Jesus Christ!

2. Content! ... The things you have heard from me ...

Paul clearly tells Timothy what he is to entrust to others by reminding him of what he had been taught by Paul himself! Fortunately for Timothy this was no mystery. Over and over again the young student of Paul heard the gospel taught in its fullness in Southern Galatia, Macedonia, and Asia. He had also heard Paul refute those who had wanted to turn it into mere legalism or empty it of its genuine meaning. Rooted in the sacrificial death of Christ, Timothy was being reminded that Christ's substitutionary death was victoriously accompanied by his resurrection from death and the grave. Without that victory over death itself, the world lies hopeless in sin.

Another thing that we must not miss here is the apostolic authority underlying the content of the teaching. Paul unashamedly says "from me." This requirement of "all things gospel" having apostolic sanction was in force until the end of the apostolic age and the initial dissemination of the completed New Testament writings. Until that point the apostles exercised gospel authority under the direct sanction of the Lord himself.

Finally, the gospel cannot be allowed to be compromised with health-and-wealth promises, flashy yet vacuous healing ministries, or my "best life now" gospels so prevalent today among false teachers. This is precisely why Paul had earlier admonished his protege to "keep a close watch on yourself and on the doctrine (teaching, 1 Tim 4:16)". Doctrine is not just part of the training protocol, it is the vital essence of it!

3. Character! ... Faithful Men ...

When a runner hands off the baton in an Olympic race, he or she has to be certain that teammates are both ready to *receive* it and will prove themselves to be *responsible* with it. Without that certainty, the race is jeopardized. Think of the countless hours a team practices the handoffs to make absolutely sure the runners are ready for race day!

Paul uses one word to describe those to whom we entrust with the gospel baton—the word *faithful*. No better word describes the inward nature or character of the person. In China, and other countries closed to the gospel and the Bible, this word describes best those who face arrest, jail, and yes, death for propagating the gospel of Jesus. In the Chinese house churches, many of these leaders cannot be entrusted with leadership unless they have paid an enormous price to prove their character in leading secret churches. Why? Because every member's life depends on the faithfulness of their leader to protect them, provide vital teaching to them, and to train other leaders who can reproduce the same training in others.

Without that kind of certainty among the leadership the entire process falls apart before it can ever get started!

4. Continuity! . . . Who will be able to teach others also . . .

What happens if, at the beginning of this entire process, we entrust the gospel to men and women who are not discerning in their choices? Let's say they make choices of people who themselves are faithful but they in turn choose those who aren't proven people of character. This means that the gospel essentially goes from being multigenerational to single-generational. That is exactly what happened in my own family. My great grandfather, who was a pastor-farmer, failed to pass the faith on to his son—my grandfather. He in turn failed to pass the faith on to his three sons—my father and two uncles. My father failed to pass the faith on to his family, which included me. Had I not heard the gospel and come to faith in Christ the cycle would have continued. However, I did hear the gospel and, after coming to faith in Christ, I have been privileged to see my four children and twelve grandchildren all come to faith in Christ as well. If my years are extended by God's grace, I will live to see if the faith, along with its doctrinal content, is passed on to my great-grandchildren. This would mean that since my father's era, four generations of those who bear both my name and, more importantly, the name of Jesus Christ have been faithful in moving and multiplying the gospel forward! That is what God commanded of us to do with this most valuable and precious commodity!

This strategic plan was to continue through Timothy, multiply through other faithful men, and then innumerable others after them through ensuring that generation after generation would have access to the gospel. This is quite the plan when you consider that, by the end of Paul's life, there were no more than ten to fifteen thousand Christians in the entire Roman Empire! This very fact underscores the enormity of what Paul is actually communicating to his beloved confidant among all his other ministry associates. We must not underestimate the content of what Paul is saying or its value for the ensuing church age. Paul is making this his last will and testament which will ultimately close his illustrious life of ministry for Jesus Christ.

However, by the end of the fourth century, the twelve apostles had become nearly thirty million followers of Christ![1] What had happened? This profound scale of growth did not and could not have occurred without exponential multiplication generationally. More importantly, it could not have happened without the training of leaders in their own locales to in turn train others. The results of Paul's method speak for themselves. By the end of that first century, the amazing movement of the gospel had significantly entered the bloodstream of the world's population.

In the following pages, you will begin to see how Paul's growth model is presently transforming the continent of Africa and is now being recognized as the essential method for the rapid extension of the gospel into the 10/40 window and beyond. However, this won't happen using graphs and charts on where Christianity has been historically or where the institutional evangelical church is presently headed. The nationals whom we have had the privilege of training and empowering over the last thirteen years will speak to you through their own testimonies. What they have to say about the perpetuation of the gospel is not only important to hear but demands to be heard by this generation. My prayer is that Paul's rallying cry to Timothy in the waning hours of his life might become ours in this generation as well.

---

1. MacMullen, *Christianizing the Roman Empire*.
The author is one of a very few that offers substantive discussion on the growth of Christianity into the fourth century, pressing more than 30 million followers. His argument for the growth in numbers rightly centers around the Roman Empire's coercion policies under Constantine, and the associated sociological factors operating under the Roman political umbrella. That being said, the overall growth numbers of worldwide Christianity cannot be attributed to only the empire itself knowing that Christianity had already found its way into Germanic regions, the continent of Africa, and India. These factors are what makes numerical preciseness so speculative in the first century.

# CHAPTER TWO

## What Is the Mission of Missions?

Do you remember the last time you had a national pastor speak at your church about the Great Commission of Christ or even worldwide missions in general? Have you ever had a national pastor from Asia, Africa, or South America in your church to talk to you about how to effectively reach their region of the world with the gospel of Jesus Christ? I would say probably not, but if you have, it was likely more of a needs-based presentation of perhaps helping with a building project, purchasing Bibles, or maybe bringing a team to assist with a Vacation Bible School or soccer camp to reach young people.

Are any of these things bad? Of course not! They are important, needed, and can always promote the gospel in some significant way! However, how many times have you had a national pastor stand in your church and ask you to help send trainers who can theologically train and equip national pastors so they can be empowered for ministry, promote church planting, and effectively reach their populations with the gospel right where they live and work? It is not a very frequent event at any of our Christ-honoring churches. However, it should be because nationals do not need language training to reach their nations. They do not require courses in cross-cultural assimilation, and they don't need directions on how to nurture and care for the people beside whom they will live and die.

## WHAT IS THE MISSION OF MISSIONS?

I was reminded of a quote attributed to Henry Ford emblazoned on the walls of his restaurant namesake, Ford's Garage. It reads: "If I had asked people what they wanted they would have said faster horses." Unfortunately, there is no evidence that Ford ever said it, but someone who understood cars, horses, and people surely did. I'm wondering if we asked the same question to most Christians about how to fulfill the Great Commission what the reply might be. I have an idea most Christian leaders would say something like: "Send more missionaries." However, is that really the answer? Would that fix the problem of how to reach between three and four billion people with the gospel? I believe that answer is simple; only if their mission is to train the nationals to do it!

Do you know that training nationals to do this very thing on their own mission fields is not only biblical, but it was precisely what Paul told Timothy to do shortly before his own martyrdom? Time and again in the book of Acts and in the Pastoral Epistles, Paul directs local leaders to carry on ministry where they both live and work. In Titus 1:5 Paul directs Titus to "appoint elders in every town." What Paul is commanding here is not just to be done in Crete but everywhere there is a need for ongoing leadership. Why? Because the entire cycle of gospel work begins with capable leadership. Once capable local leadership is trained and established, the cycle of training others, starting new churches, and doing vigorous evangelism can take place indefinitely.

One of our Tanzanian trainers recently reported:

> The excitement of our now-trained pastors is beyond words and our training has deeply encouraged multiple other pastors, promoted indigenous church planting, but most of all, it has brought evangelism to levels we have never seen before now.

(See Pastor H.'s story at the end of this chapter.)

I want you to notice something critically important about this process. First, notice that Paul did not suggest bringing in pastors or evangelists from Western Macedonia, Corinth, or Philippi. He didn't ask the church in Iconium or Lystra to pray about being missionaries in Crete. He didn't ask the Ephesian elders to pack their bags and move to an island far removed from their culture and life experience to become Cretans. We might ask the question, "Why would Paul invite Greek-speaking, large-city urbanites to minister on a small island that spoke a different dialect?"

Exactly! Paul did what was the most effective and normal thing possible. *He equipped those who spoke the local language, understood the culture, and cared most about their populace to reach their own locale for Jesus Christ.*

For decades, I have watched churches send out missionary couples to the far reaches of our world who have surrendered their lives to evangelize or start new church plants in areas of need. In most cases, these willing individuals, couples, and families were not anything like the people, places, or cultures they were preparing to enter. Usually, they were required to begin language studies immediately upon arrival on the field. Learning the language for missionaries is time-consuming, expensive, and tedious. It requires anywhere from 3–5 years for them to master the language suitably for conversational purposes and yet, even then, they will never be able to communicate on the level of a natural born citizen. Added to that is the reality that up to half of most Western missionaries do not remain on the field longer than 3–5 years.[2]

One of our Global Baptist Training Foundation (GBTF) African trainers has commented:

> Foreign missionaries, despite their best efforts, often require years to learn a language fluently, and even then, they may struggle with local dialects, expressions, and idioms. This language gap limits their effectiveness compared to national pastors, who can preach, counsel, and disciple seamlessly in their native tongues without the need for translation.

(Pastor Z. elected not to submit his personal story.)

Once again, when we look at the pattern of the NT practices of Paul, we don't see him introducing cultural foreigners into areas to do ministry. Just the opposite. Paul mitigated these kinds of issues so that the missionaries themselves would not become an issue!

2. Yohannan, *Come, Let's Reach the World*, 45.

## WHAT IS THE MISSION OF MISSIONS?

On the occasion that Paul brought Timothy into the mission team while in Southern Galatia, he forced Timothy to be circumcised so that his religious background would not be unnecessarily offensive to their Jewish audiences. Paul understood that language, cultural, and personal barriers to the gospel had to be eliminated or minimized at the very least so that the gospel would not be hindered. This is such a key component of cultural acceptance of both the messenger and message of the gospel that it is simply hard to miss. Once a national can reenter their ministries with theological preparation, there is no one more qualified to communicate the gospel in a cultural setting. Listen to this pastor:

> I believe GBTF on-site training works for us nationals because we already know the languages and dialects of our people. No one can communicate the gospel and biblical truth to our own people like we can. They get this like no one else. GBTF is training nationals like us to train other nationals, and it is working powerfully. (See Pastor C. M.'s story at the end of this chapter.)

## WE NEED TO ASK OURSELVES, WHAT IS THE ULTIMATE PURPOSE OF THE MISSIONARY?

Let's directly answer that question by saying that no matter whether you are an administrative helper, ministry facilitator, teacher, or church planter, you are there to make the gospel known, help start churches among new believers, and disciple and train leaders to pastor new churches and then reproduce that model over and over again.

If existing Christian believers are available to be trained and taught, then our focus can be directed on equipping them to reach and train others to church plant and evangelize. Two concepts taught in most missions-related training courses need to be reassessed to better serve the nationals.

The first concept is *cross-cultural communication*. In a pioneer mission situation, learning the language is absolutely key to making the gospel known. An unreached people group (UPG) must be able to understand every nuance of the gospel in their mother tongue. They also must be able to read the Scripture in their native language if they are going to be able to come to faith in Christ. Only then can they, in turn, train someone else in gospel essentials. Although not impossible, it is nearly out of the realm of possibility that any outsider to a culture and language would be able to communicate on the level of a local indigenous person. However, if the mission situation is not pioneer in nature but rather perpetuating the gospel through trained nationals, why must we insist on trying to master the language ourselves?

For nearly fourteen years we have taught existing believers on the ground all over the globe through gifted translators. These translators are often the most capable communicators of any given culture. For years I have noticed that my translators are able to inject more nuance, meaning, and energy into my teaching than my teaching is actually producing itself! That is the power not only of good *translation* but powerful and effective *communication*!

The second concept is *cross-cultural assimilation*. In pioneer mission situations, this helps any missionary family understand what it will mean for them to fit into an existing culture. Because the mission is to be able to relate both socially and culturally, knowing *how to not stick out like a sore thumb* is highly important for casual acceptance. Assimilation means that we essentially become as invisible as we possibly can in order to identify *within* a culture. However, here is the problem that never goes away for any missionary anywhere in the world. *Identifying* with the culture never equals becoming *invisible* within the culture! You could live fifty years in a foreign culture and still not be assimilated as a national!

So what is the best solution for overcoming the problems of communication and assimilation? I believe that the answer lies in how we understand our job in the first place. If we understand our job as either a pioneer to a UPG or as one perpetuating the gospel by training existing believers on the ground, the goal remains the same for both models. *It has to end up in training the national to train other nationals!*

However, many missionaries may not have a clear understanding or strategy for carrying out this process. How we choose to carry out that process in areas where there may be believers who desire training can greatly vary. No one gets this better than the national who is the target audience on which our mission efforts are focused.

In every focus group we have ever done to date, the nationals want one thing more than anything else they could receive from us, and that is theological training for ministry. Before we consider the need to change the way we understand and practice missions in our local churches, let's consider what missions may look like in many churches today.

## WHAT IS THE COST OF THIS?

Our traditional methods are extremely demanding and costly to say the least.

Depending on the nature of denominational requirements for sending missionaries, the initial demands can look quite different. This varies among Evangelical churches, but generally, most missionaries, other than Southern Baptists, are required to raise their own support among member churches. This can be and oftentimes is very tough, and can now take up to five years or more to accomplish. It requires a lot of travel, vehicle maintenance, and wear and tear upon young families. But we must also consider the hidden costs for husband and wife, the kids, and their upbringing/schooling, etc. Then think about how many thousands of dollars are required to maintain this process for five years or more! Stay with me. Consider also that most traditional couples who go permanently to live in Europe, Africa, or South America are raising support to maintain a home, a vehicle, schooling, food costs, insurances, and whatever else is fundamentally necessary for living in a foreign country. These costs range anywhere from $6,000 to $10,000 a month depending on location and country. That requires a lot of investment and effort for a long time just to be able to go to a mission field! One of our West African trainers responded by saying:

> For less than a tenth of the cost of maintaining a Western missionary family, an indigenous family can live and function normally and yet do ten times the work. (See Pastor P. W.'s story at the end of this chapter.)

Consider two areas affecting every local church which is involved in fulfilling the Great Commission of Christ.

First let's consider the *spiritual impact* of the present system of sending out missionary couples to mission fields that are outside the 10/40 window.[3] These mission fields are typically no longer pioneer areas for the gospel, and yet we are treating them as such. Wouldn't we be more strategic in approach by identifying "Christian people groups" in areas like this to train them to reach their areas, regions, and ultimately their nations?

In the hallways and vestibules of many of our churches we can see and read the mission letters of hundreds of missionary couples who have surrendered to go to a foreign mission field. In these letters you will read countless stories of language school difficulties, housing problems, health issues, efforts to buy land for a church, individuals requiring prayer for salvation, physical healing, etc. All these micro-stories associated with missionary life are real and justified. Each month comes and goes and there is a salvation here and a baptism there. There are Vacation Bible Schools, soccer camps, and Bible studies.

What is the elephant in this room? What is the real focus that we should want to see and hear about in all our mission letters from every missionary or missions family from which we receive correspondence? Perhaps you have gotten my point already. We

---

[3]. The 10/40 window is the rectangular area of North Africa, the Middle East, and Asia, approximately between ten degrees north and forty degrees north latitude. The 10/40 window includes the majority of the world's Muslims, Hindus, and Buddhists, comprising about two-thirds of the world population who have never heard the gospel. Most of the governments of these people groups directly or indirectly oppose Christian missionaries and the gospel of Christ.

## WHAT IS THE MISSION OF MISSIONS?

should be hearing about the progress being made in training the nationals to reach their areas, regions, and nations for Christ! That is the bulls-eye we should be aiming at in our efforts. Everything done must be connected to that target of training and equipping the indigenous believers!

Now, what is the *spiritual impact* of this upon a congregation when the bulls-eye is being consistently missed or ignored, perhaps for decades and even generations within local churches? I can tell you that it is stifling. Quietly and consistently, mission interests retreat. What was once the most exciting enterprise of local church life and fellowship becomes just another thing we do at church. It can be disconnected from what really excites us. We may have more joy about the excitement of the Sunday morning worship, small group ministry growth, or the Friday night fish fry, none of which are bad in themselves *if connected to moving and multiplying the gospel forward*. That being said, global evangelism trumps them all because Jesus clearly commanded us to reach all people with the gospel of his Son.

Have you ever been in a church where nothing is more important than reaching the world with the life-changing gospel of Christ? It is truly something to behold! Do you know why? It puts everyone on the same page spiritually. It establishes the ultimate goal of why everyone is coming! Whether you are walking to a Bible study class or the main service, the theme of being on mission dots every "I" and crosses every "T." It also causes all members to evaluate themselves in light of what is most important. If you have ever been involved in a new, growing business, you might begin to understand what I'm getting at here. When a new business is successful in selling its product and making money, everyone on board is excited because the ultimate purpose of the organization is being reached! In a local church this kind of visceral energy produces spiritual growth and becomes a magnet for both internal and external expansion within a church. Why? Because the church is fulfilling the ultimate purpose for which it exists, and its subsequent spiritual life directly reflects it! Once that becomes the ethos of a church, that church is the most exciting place to be any day of the week.

I remember years ago, when I was in seminary, we had a class on church growth and administration. In one of our class sessions, we were asked to write out a purpose statement for our church or prospective church that would spell out why our particular church existed. It was an interesting project because there was a word limit of 8–12 words. Some students were able to do it, but many others found it difficult to verbalize the spiritual purpose of their church in such brief terms. Long and difficult statements were finally whittled down to such statements like "Making disciples for Christ here and around the world." The point of the exercise was to force each of us to know what we were aiming at.

Let's face it, there are countless good things that we can do in Christ's name that are all good. Pregnancy centers, food banks, clothing ministries, addiction and rehabilitation centers, grief management. The list is really endless because human needs are endless. However, just like those brief eight-to-ten-word purpose statements, we need to have a target that is only the size of the Great Commission. Jesus didn't give us numerous targets, but He did give us one, and that is to make disciples both where we are now and extending out to the farthest reaches of our world. When we tie the purpose of making disciples to everything else we do in Christ's name, it all works. If, however, we allow everything else we do in Christ's name to supplant or ignore our key purpose of making disciples, we have made the good things to become an enemy of the best thing. Equipping national believers to make disciples where they live is the true bullseye!

Now consider the *financial impact* of a poor mission policy upon the local church and its missionaries. Consider that for typical independent churches, support per missionary varies from $100 to $250 a month. Churches will usually attempt to be minimally involved in as many missionary efforts as possible to generate a global footprint for the church. However, when most mission families require in excess of $6,000 monthly to live on a mission field, that demands that mission families have no less than forty churches supporting $150 each monthly. Most mission families will have to visit nearly three hundred churches in a three-to-five-year period to generate a minimum of $6,000 a month.

For independent missionaries, the math is not encouraging for a timely departure to the field. During this process, there is inestimable time, effort, money, and human sacrifice in a process that is designed only to pay living expenses. It cannot assist with any of the intangibles like knowing the host language or culture, which in the end are the fundamentals for spiritual success. That is why training nationals is so critical. They are resident experts in both the language and culture!

Pastor FSL, who is a trainer in a closed country formerly open to missionaries, responded by saying:

> I saw the financial report of a missionary in our area that spent over $8,000 a month just to live in our country with his family with only five children. They don't know the language or culture that well and it makes it hard for them to be truly effective here. However, we could entirely support the families of over fifty church planters with that amount of money. I don't understand this thinking.

(See FSL's story at the end of this chapter.)

When you consider that a typical missionary family has spent as much as 3–5 years just raising the money to get to their mission, is it any wonder that this affects their longevity? Add to this the real possibility that they are not laser-focused on reaching and training nationals to ultimately reach their own and you have a recipe for minimal impact. That may be what then becomes the greatest impediment to the local church in general. After all the time, effort, and money invested in so many missionaries whose monthly letters reflect minimal impact, the general missions malaise will naturally follow.

In the financial investment world, we use a term which identifies how valuable our investment becomes over time. It's called our "return of investment," or "ROI." Financial investors anywhere in the world pay close attention at the end of every quarter of the year to make sure they are maximizing the ROI in their portfolio. If one stock is not making sufficient gains or even failing, they will sell that stock and reinvest in another stock which will pay better dividends. Anyone who invests in stock simply will not tolerate a stock which either loses money or doesn't make any money at all. Even Jesus used a parable to illustrate this principle in Matt 25:14–30, called "the parable of the talents."

Jesus told the story of a landowner who called his three servants and left his property for them to manage in his absence. He gave one servant five talents, another two talents, and another one talent. Then he left on his journey, expecting them to take care of his investment by increasing its value while he was gone. The one with five talents immediately went out and traded in the market and made five talents more. He literally doubled the original investment. The one with two talents did the same and doubled his investment. The third servant decided that he would do nothing with his master's money and simply chose to bury it in the ground until his master returned. When the master returned from his long journey, he met with his servants to find out how they did with the money he invested with each of them. He was very satisfied with the first two servant's ROI because they had managed their investments quite well, even doubling the original amount. When the master came to the third servant and found out what he had done (or not done) with his talents, he was very angry with that servant. The master was not upset with the servant because he had invested unwisely or even stolen the talent. He was angry because he had simply chosen to do the easiest possible thing—nothing at all. He had chosen to not risk any time, effort, or thought into the investment he had been entrusted with by his master. He had taken the easy way out and done nothing!

Remember there will always be some risk involved when investing in anything! There is the risk of time, effort, market ups and downs, etc. It takes faith, wisdom, and a lot of prayer to ensure that our investments in God's business are well managed! Just remember that our investments as believers involve lost people, and, at the judgment seat of Christ, many believers will discover

## WHAT IS THE MISSION OF MISSIONS?

that they made bad investments and lost every bit of their reward! Others will lose some of what they could have had, and others who invested carefully and managed well will be rewarded well. That is the law of ROI!

Churches are also investing valuable kingdom assets. The missions budget of every church reflects what the membership is investing for the advancement of the gospel around the world. How is that money being invested? In whom is the church trusting to maximize their investments so that they realize the greatest ROI possible? These are questions every church mission's committee needs to answer before they can maximize their investments! Many churches today are not giving sufficient time, effort, or thought into their eternal investment program of global missions. A poor mission's policy will have a negative *financial impact* that will last far longer than any of us realize.

## WHAT ABOUT THAT NEW CULTURE?

Remember, potential missionaries are being immersed into a cultural environment that is likely completely foreign to them. One thing is for certain. No matter how long they live in that culture they will always be considered outsiders by those who are native to that area. I have served for twenty years as a missionary church planter in another country. From the day I arrived in that distinct culture until the day I departed, I was always seen as the American citizen I am. I tried to blend in, follow the cultural trends, and use local terminology, but I couldn't suitably erase my identity enough for it to disappear. Any person who is passionate about reaching a particular culture understands what I am talking about here, and I think it is to be expected. Every day I got up, and everywhere I went, I was who I was in their eyes.

I remember in my first missions experience in a maritime province of Canada, I thought a lobster trap decorating my front porch would help me identify as a local. I probably should have checked out the other porches in my neighborhood before doing that, but I didn't. Well, one day the mailman asked me why

I had that ugly thing on my front porch. Unfortunately, I never completely accepted my fate and continued to double down in my efforts to become culturally invisible.

This is not unusual behavior for missionaries no matter where God has called them to minister; in fact, it's surprisingly normal. You would expect long-term foreigners in any culture to do the same thing. It makes perfect sense and certainly would engender a certain level of respect from the local population. When the gospel was first taken to China by Hudson Taylor, we all remember that he was a true pioneer missionary. Mr. Taylor wore the traditional clothing of the local population, he ate the same food, and he lived exactly as the locals lived. In that way he was able to find common ground with the Chinese that allowed him the opportunity to build trust and then relationships with the local residents, resulting in them coming to faith in Christ.

The word of God was translated in the local dialect and the work prospered. What most people don't know is that Taylor believed in training the indigenous Chinese to plant and pastor churches in all of the provinces of China, not just in the coastal areas. His legacy was not necessarily in what he personally had done but what he had trained the indigenous Christians to do. The results were incredibly successful. Both the timing and the methods of Taylor were extremely providential because in 1891, just fourteen years before he died, the Boxer Rebellion took place which forced nearly all of the British and American missionary personnel out of the country. However, because the nationals had been trained and prepared, the work of the gospel carried forward. Despite the dismantling of churches and the forced eradication of Christianity at large by Communist dictators, there remains in China today a vast underground network of committed believers in Jesus Christ in the house church movement. It is hard to imagine these present phenomena being totally disconnected to the foundations laid by Taylor. The fertile ground for the gospel had not been totally plowed under by a hostile government.

Here's the singular point of Taylor's story. His determination to assimilate into the culture was not an attempt to become

## WHAT IS THE MISSION OF MISSIONS?

culturally invisible to them. It was so he could have their respect and trust, which would enable him to give them the gospel of Christ. Once they came to faith, he placed the mantle of responsibility for reaching China on them as independent emissaries of the truth. They bore the full responsibility for passing the baton to others, who would in turn do the same.

The fact is, the Hudson Taylor pioneer paradigm worked not necessarily because Taylor identified so closely with the Chinese culture of his day, but because *he understood that the longevity of his mission had to be rooted in training and empowering the indigenous Chinese people.* This much is certain in spreading the gospel: we have to meet people where they are as they are if we going to impact them. Because the gospel is a supernatural reality, it logically transcends any culture or cultural issue. Our job as God's messengers is to make the gospel known. Culture and language are huge issues, but they certainly are not insurmountable barriers if you don't you master them.

Think of the issue of culture, language, and race in Acts 8 with the Ethiopian eunuch. The eunuch came from an area in Egypt known as the Kingdom of Cush, a totally Black race. It was a place whose religion was derived from solar worship and whose language would have been foreign to Hebrew-speaking Jews from Jerusalem. He was a God-fearer who would have not have been allowed in the temple areas as a gentile, not to mention a likely physical eunuch. He was from a place in Africa alongside the Nile that was on the outer reaches of the civilized world.[4]

Philip, on the other hand, was a born Jew from Jerusalem who spoke both Greek and Hebrew fluently. God directs the deacon Philip, who had been in a great revival among the Samaritans, to go to Gaza to meet this African eunuch. The eunuch likely does not speak or read Hebrew, at least not very well, if at all. He is riding along in his chariot near Gaza attempting to read and make sense of a copy of Isaiah from the Greek translation of Isaiah called the Septuagint. He is reading, but not understanding, the text and Philip, anticipating this by the Spirit's prompting, asks him if he

4. Polhill, *Acts*, 223.

comprehends the text. The eunuch basically says he would not be able to understand it without guidance. Philip then explains the meaning of the text in full.

You talk about a clash of culture, language, and race! These two individuals could not have been any further apart culturally, racially, and even linguistically. However, Philip remedies the situation by simply making the Greek text of the Hebrew Bible plain and understood to this distant traveler, who likely read and spoke the market language of the Koine Greek dialect as well. This was the singular point of common ground. Make no mistake, this was an advantage to Philip in communicating the truth of Scripture to the Eunuch! *But, there was absolutely no cultural or racial common ground.* They could not have been any more different in those two key areas. Philip could do nothing but assist the eunuch at the only point of contact they shared: *the understanding of the word of God.* When he does what only he could do at the request of the eunuch, God opened his eyes to the gospel from Isa 53:7-8. Once the eunuch was converted and sent home a believer, we have every reason to believe he reached his city and culture with the gospel!

Here's the point. If missionaries perceive themselves as having to fit in in order to be accepted, or for the gospel to be accepted, they will never be able to fully accomplish their task. However, if mission personnel simply see themselves as those who are there to assist local believers and effectively understand and communicate the word of God, the perception completely changes. But not only does it change for them, it changes for those they are there to reach and train with the gospel. It actually frees the trainer to be completely transparent, and this is a vital element of any training process. Perhaps you are now asking, "How can we change this perception of having to fit in or identify with a culture in order to reach it?"

What if missionaries began to simply see themselves as trainers of those faithful Christians in a culture to become trainers themselves? Isn't this what Paul commanded Timothy to do in Ephesus? If that were the case, is it possible that local translators could be used to facilitate theological learning so the burdens of arduous language training could be averted indefinitely? Might it be possible to set up quarterly training sessions on-site for a few weeks every quarter or two coupled with Zoom meetings, emails, and texts in between? We have been doing just that for well over a decade, and I can testify to you that language barriers have never been a factor in the training process. Through the use of good local translators, the passing on of the training along with personal communication has happened flawlessly. There are two elements of this process which assure a clear communication process.

The first is having a local person fluent in English to translate the teaching materials into the host language. We currently have fifteen courses (with more to come), so by the time the students finish the entire series of classes, all the subjects are translated and can be duplicated permanently by the student trainers as they teach others. This can be costly at the beginning of any training classroom, but it never needs to be done twice.

The second element is that of finding a good local translator for the classroom. That individual must be a believer, and he or she should also be an experienced communicator of the local language or dialect! When you have both elements in place, the communication of the materials and impact upon the students is measurably heightened. For more than a decade, we have watched this process turn large classrooms of untrained indigenous pastors and wives into passionate ambassadors of the gospel. The result? These trained nationals have started nearly 1,600 churches and reached tens of thousands of their own populations with the gospel of Christ. They are truly living out each day the reality of the Great Commission and what is the essence of the *mission* of missions.

## PASTOR H.

> I was raised in a pagan family. My father had two wives who both were idol worshipers. They forced us to worship in the traditional way of the Nyakyusa tribe.

Pastor H. was born on February 5, 1966, in the Ikama village in the Mbeya region of Tanzania. It was one of many idol-worshiping villages, not only in his own region, but the entire country of Tanzania. Pastor H. had no say in the worship traditions of his family or his village. The village chief was in absolute control over the families of his village as well as the spiritual life. The two could not be separated. The fact that his father had come from the traditional worship of his parents only deepened the darkness in which the family lived in H.'s adolescent upbringing. The dual roles of his father's wives would have been cruelly oppressive for any young man, and H. was no exception.

As Pastor H. grew up in the bondage of pagan life, he became what he described as

> a very quiet and angry individual capable of harming others. This is what I learned through the example of my family, and although I knew I was a dangerous soul I did not know how to change or be different than what I had become.

In 1984, at the age of eighteen, H. was almost ready to finish the Ikama Primary School in his village when one day an American missionary came to his school to preach the gospel of Christ to the students. That particular day the preacher spoke from John 3:16, sharing the message of God's boundless love for sinners from the Scriptures. He emphasized not only the eternal love of God but also the eternal nature of separation from God in hell. He had never heard the Scriptures before and yet he knew that he had heard truth that was most certainly from the God of creation, and now his own possible salvation from sin. H. proclaimed:

> I made a life-changing decision to accept Jesus Christ as my Lord and Savior, even though I knew in my heart that my decision put me in jeopardy of my life itself. Just a few days later, my father and my two mothers disowned me and I was forced to leave and go far from my home and live in the bush where I slept in a tree. On the morning of the seventh day my father gave his own life to Christ and sent a house servant to bring me back home.

Pastor H.'s family joined a church outside his village and moved to the capitol of Dar Es Salaam. There H. met and married his wife who has been his steadfast partner now for over thirty years. They have raised a godly family whose children all serve the Lord in the church he pastors in the capitol.

When we met Pastor H. in 2021, I noticed that the Tanzanian classroom of students was not only progressing rapidly, but they deeply desired to begin spreading the GBTF program throughout the country's network of Baptist churches. With the help of another ministry trainer, we managed to graduate this group in just over a two-year period and see them continue to multiply themselves exponentially. Today there are seven Tanzanian trainers who are multiplying classrooms in every region of the country.

This has resulted in the planting of scores of churches and the training of hundreds of pastors and church leaders.

Pastor H. adds:

> Global Baptist Training Foundation has demonstrated great success through its approach of focusing on nationals being trained to do what only Western missionaries once did. The excitement of our pastors is high, and our training has encouraged multiple other pastors and promoted indigenous church planting, but most of all, it has brought evangelism to levels we have never seen before now.

## PASTOR C. N.

> No one can communicate the gospel and biblical truth to our own people like we can.

C. was born June 15, 1985, in Commune Matongo Province in the country of Burundi. His father was a deacon in a small Baptist church in his village, and he would later become the pastor of the church shortly before 2000. The war would not end until 2005.

Burundi is surrounded by the Democratic Republic of Congo, Tanzania, and Rwanda. It gained its independence from Belgium in 1960 and has since then been one of the poorest and least developed of any African country. Like many of its neighbors Burundi has suffered through civil war and political instability almost from the beginning of its gaining independence.

Eight-year-old C. told how God spared his life at the beginning of the civil war in 1993. He recalled the following scene:

> One night my sisters and I were lying in bed when we heard the guns shooting. The rebels were near our house shouting and burning down the schoolhouses when they knocked at our door demanding us to open. We were frozen in fear because our mother and father had fled believing rebels would allow us to live if found alone. My sisters and I quickly climbed under the bed when suddenly the door was broken down and the rebels entered. They took everything in the house but did not find us under the bed. They set fire to our dwelling but somehow the part of the house where we were hiding did not catch fire and we were spared. God had spared me from death to be his servant.

Young C. and his two sisters were later reunited with their mother and father, and, in 2000, at the age of fifteen, C. became a believer in Jesus Christ and was baptized upon the profession of his faith. Believers in Burundi are required to have a certain amount of biblical training after they come to faith in Christ to be baptized and join the church. This training has proven to be instrumental to the churches we have encountered in our training regimen in Burundi.

Pastors who come for theological training are highly motivated, self-reliant, and determined to access our biblical training at any cost to themselves. Even though they live in an impoverished country, they always contribute what they have for feeding themselves during each training week rather than relying on their teaching hosts.

Consequently, these Burundi pastors and church leaders have demonstrated a deep spiritual commitment to GBTF values beyond their theological training. They lead Africa in starting churches, evangelism, and have a passion for training others. C., like his Christian countrymen, seems to instinctively understand that once trained, he will be able to leverage his training for the kingdom of God.

He said:

> I believe GBTF works for us nationals because we already know the languages and dialects of our people. No one can communicate the gospel and biblical truth to our own people like we can. They get this like no one else. GBTF is training nationals like us to train other nationals, and it is working powerfully.

## PASTOR P. W.

> For less than a tenth of the cost of maintaining a Western missionary family, an indigenous family can live and function normally and do ten times the work.

Pastor P. W. is one of our most active and capable of all of our GBTF coordinators. He loves to work and see the spiritual results of his labor. When I first met him in 2017 in Gbarga, Liberia, he was struggling to maintain the health clinic compound on which GBTF held its initial classrooms. The PA clinic was being superintended by a Western missionary who did not allow the nationals he had helped train and supervise to take full control of the day-to-day operations. Neither would he entrust them with the financial resources necessary for them to be independent of US oversight. He was frustrated and yet found working with our training organization an opportunity for service he truly enjoyed and found gratifying.

We began with about seventy pastors in 2017 and met in a small building and crammed classroom for two full years. As our classroom sizes grew and the theological impact continued among the pastors who gathered twice a year, P.'s PA operation took a turn for the better. Through a series of apparent setbacks the clinic was forced to assume control over what appeared to be a dying enterprise upon the sudden decision by the US missionary to end his work in Gbarnga. Surprisingly, P. and his other Liberian assistants found a way to build the clinic's student base and recover their financial footing. Within three years the clinic became both profitable and highly productive throughout central Liberia all without the influx of any US support. This was an interesting turn of events in light of what GBTF was attempting to do at the same time in empowering national pastors to assume full responsibility for reaching their nations.

During this same period Global Baptist Training Foundation surpassed one hundred pastors being trained, and by 2022 we were able to graduate our first GBTF class. These men went on to launch well over two hundred new church plants in the process. By this date in March of 2025 that number of new church plants started by GBTF-trained pastors has exceeded six hundred in Liberia alone. It has been truly astounding to witness what God has done through these nationals empowered by their classroom training for ministry.

P. W. was born on July 4, 1977, in U-Lah Town, a bush community in the Kokoyah District of Bong County, Liberia. In 1988, when P. was eleven years old, a Baptist missionary came to his area and presented the gospel to the entire village. That day he believed the gospel, along with a great number of his fellow villagers. He remembered it as "a joyful day."

Within a year the nation became embroiled in civil war and things, by P.'s own account, "became very complicated for me and our family."

On December 24, one day before Christmas in 1989, P. was forced to leave his mother and father and seek refuge in the Ivory Coast, a neighboring West African country. He would never see his mother again. Because there was no functional hospital in Liberia at the time, she died from complications from dehydration.

Nearly a decade later, in 1998, P. returned to Liberia to his home village and the church of U-lah Town. With little remaining of what once was his home, he moved and relocated to Gbarga in central Liberia, where he met and married his wife. They now have

# WHAT IS THE MISSION OF MISSIONS?

a family of five children including three boys and two girls. They started a new church in Gbarnga, and soon thereafter, he began his medical training as a PA under his American missionary PA instructor.

Today, P. continues to manage the health clinic but also deeply enjoys his ministry with Global Baptist Training Foundation as our West African coordinator. He oversees over six hundred churches and is directly involved in opening adjacent countries to GBTF in training nationals. Much of what he knows he has learned through the crucible of difficult life experiences, and he understands the distinct advantages of empowering nationals in reaching their own nations for Christ.

Not only are nationals more capable because of their expertise in the local dialects and culture, but Pastor P. says:

> For less than a tenth of the cost of maintaining a Western missionary family, an indigenous family can live and function normally and yet do ten times the work.

## PASTOR M. S. L.

> My vision is to see within ten years all of the ten states of South Sudan evangelized with 2–3 new churches in each state pastored by men trained with GBTF materials. My family and I have dedicated ourselves to full-time ministry in South Sudan in order to see God do this.

M. S. L. was born in a refugee camp during the SPLM Civil War that ultimately led to the independence of South Sudan. He did not know the exact date of his birth. He was the second born in a family of nine children: seven boys and two girls. His parents were Christians and attended a Baptist church in the immediate area where S. went to church every Sunday. He thought himself to be a genuine Christian until one day S. realized he was a lost sinner for whom Jesus had died. He trusted Christ as his Savior on December 11, 2008. Three days later he submitted himself for baptism and was called soon thereafter to become a children's teacher.

## Voices of the Nationals

The Lord greatly used S., and he began to open children's Bible clubs in Kajo-keji and in the many villages. When his father opened a new church plant in the town of Yei, Pastor S went with him and opened fourteen Bible clubs all over the city. He began to be noticed by the National Security Service (NSS). They began to "attend" the meetings S. held among the young people. They believed that S. was recruiting young men for the rebel groups opposing the South Sudanese government. During this difficult period, many of the young men S. trained with the word of God were arrested and forced to join the South Sudanese army, and others were never seen again.

Because of the chaos the NSS was causing, his father encouraged S. to flee South Sudan and go to Uganda to live. This advice saved S's life. A few years later he returned to South Sudan. Not long after he returned S's father died, and God brought a man into Samuel's life who would prove to be a significant influence. His name was J. L. N.

Between 2004 and 2016, J. started thirty-four new churches in Uganda and South Sudan. His dying prayer was that his church planting ministry would not die with him but continue on into the future. When S. was notified of his death, he decided to call a prayer meeting and encourage the men to fast and pray so they would know how to move forward. Among five key points of prayer S. outlined at the time was the need for all the pastors to receive biblical training.

M. S. L. later reported the results of his prayer request:

> It took only three weeks for the Lord to answer my prayer. A man who was a friend to Pastor J. came to my place and I shared with him my prayer requests. He immediately introduced me to Pastor N. who invited me to the GBTF classroom in Entebbe. Though it was expensive to travel to attend this class, I sold my computer to provide my transportation to the class.

Once S. joined the Entebbe class, he immediately told the class how God had answered his prayer to provide training. S. finished his studies and has since been pouring into his South Sudanese students the same things he himself has learned.

I will never forget his testimony to the class the night of his arrival in Entebbe and how thankful he was for what he saw as a move of God in his life and in the lives of South Sudanese believers he would eventually train. However, the greatest memory will be to look back one day and see the exponential multiplication which began with the theological training of just this one national. He is planting churches all throughout South Sudan among the refugee population.

# CHAPTER THREE

## Contemporary Missions: Two Key Questions

EACH ONE OF THE following questions is relevant in carrying out our mission if there is going to be both short-term and long-term success in expanding the kingdom of God through indigenous believers. If we don't answer these questions on the front end of the process, the product will reveal we missed something that is key to world evangelization.

### 1. WHAT IS THE INITIAL PURPOSE OF THE MISSIONARY: PIONEER OR PERPETUATION?

Simply put, the missionary's purpose on earth is to extend the gospel of Christ in areas where it does not exist as a pioneer[1] to an unreached people group (UPG), or in where it exists, perpetuating it through existing believers. If the latter is the case, a missionary

---

1. The term "pioneer missionary" refers to someone who takes the gospel to entirely unreached people groups. This mission historically has involved the translation of Scripture into the native tongue, a prolonged period of learning how to communicate the language, and then living out the gospel in what often was a hostile environment because of the religious and sociological factors involved. Such pioneer missionaries as Hudson Taylor, Adoniram Judson, David Brainerd, and David Livingstone typify the pioneer missionary.

## CONTEMPORARY MISSIONS: TWO KEY QUESTIONS

doesn't need to identify within the culture but to identify those who are already in the culture who can be trained to reach others. This is the gospel reality whether someone's mission is reaching an unreached people group or in training existing believers. In either case, the ultimate purpose of missions is in training nationals to train nationals!

In a culture where the gospel does not exist, the pioneer missionary must translate the Scripture into the mother tongue. Then someone must learn that language so the gospel can be heard. Even then, once people have been evangelized, the process should lead to the teaching, training, and empowering of nationals to carry on the ministry themselves perpetually. Unless and until this is done, the pioneer method will fail in the absence of properly trained local leadership.

Since the eighteenth-century revivalist tradition, the modern missions movement practiced the Great Commission of Christ by essentially following the pioneer pattern. I shared the example of Hudson Taylor in China in the previous chapter. There was also Adoniram Judson, the first American missionary to leave America's shores in 1812, opening Burma to the gospel. In his wake, hundreds of faithfully trained nationals continued their work for decades. The pioneer method opened much of our globe to the gospel of Jesus Christ and established Christianity through local churches and trained local leaders.

As Evangelical churches continued a strong missions emphasis in the twentieth century we once again saw a vigorous response to world evangelization. Mission agencies proliferated among many conservative groups, and new efforts were being made to advance the gospel. Much of this was multidenominational, non-denominational, as well as intra-denominational in scope with many groups demonstrating multifaceted ministry interests.

Consequently, it is common today to see Christian couples in our twenty-first-century churches raising support to go to Africa, South America, Canada, Mexico, Australia, and many other global areas that already have existing believers on the ground that do not require the pioneer method to reach them with the gospel. Rather, the national believers already there simply need to be theologically and practically trained and empowered to reach their own "Jerusalem" with the gospel of Jesus Christ. They will then start new churches, reaching their own people with the gospel, who can in turn be trained to reach others.

Because we have recognized the superior ability of the indigenous believers to effectively reach their own people, equipping them and empowering them fuels the missions endeavor and assures an infinitely greater success rate. Working among their own people allows for a transparent and mutually edifying result!

Pastor N. R., a GBTF national instructor, said:

> When national trainers train national trainees, real discipleship takes place because the trainer and the trainee speak the same tongue; they share the same culture and worldview; and they face similar challenges which allows for normal relatability and problem solving.
> (See Pastor N. R.'s story at the end of this chapter.)

Another amazing possibility is that it may not require a permanent transfer of the missionary or couple to that foreign location! Now before you gasp from that statement, allow me to explain what it means. There are two serious factors which mitigate against missionaries living on the field as their permanent residence in the twenty-first century. The first is *access*. This is not as certain a possibility as it was twenty-five years ago. This is increasingly true in Muslim-dominated countries. European countries, though Christian in name, are much less tolerant to American evangelicals than ever because of extreme secularism and cultural indifference.

The second factor is *cost*. Living expenses are a significant draw on critical mission resources.

These two issues become even more relevant as we consider gospel strategies for advancing the gospel into the 10/40 window. However, if the gospel of Christ already exists in any geographical location, we must approach the mission differently by focusing on training those on the ground. Wherever we find and can locate indigenous believers in these unreached areas, we must strive to identify them and train them to reach their populations with the gospel. This aligns with Paul's principle of foundation-building. In Rom 15:20–21 the apostle said:

> And thus I make it my ambition to preach the gospel, not where Christ has already been named, lest I build on someone else's foundation, but as it is written, "Those who have never been told of him will see, and those who have never heard will understand." (ESV)

Why would we go into an area where there are existing believers and start a new church plant having a *pioneer* mindset? Why build a new foundation where one for perpetuating the gospel already exists? It doesn't make sense, does it? These believers do not require evangelism, they require training so they can become the evangelists! This is the access point for training the indigenous. Much of the inertia slowing evangelism and church planting in multiple areas of the planet evaporates when nationals are theologically trained and equipped.

## 2. WHAT TRAINING DO MISSIONARIES NEED?

There are only two important kinds of training a missionary requires for service: *theological* and *practical*. In reality, this is what any pastor or teacher must have before entering their work. We always say to our trainers: "You can't teach what you don't know."

Missionaries require *theological training* as an absolute prerequisite for preaching and teaching anywhere in the world. Proper training will determine your overall effectiveness for ministry life. Because you can never teach what you haven't learned, many of our national pastors feel hamstrung because they either do not have access to theological training or they couldn't afford it if they did. The consequences of this are devastating for both a confident and constructive ministry. In the absence of academic and practical training, pastors will often mimic the cliched examples they see on TV or hear on the radio. They will use crowd-stimulating one-liners geared at getting emotional responses. When you hear them, you immediately can recognize their similarity to how the "faith healers" and other deliverance ministers interact with their audiences. Their "mentors" are usually the personal examples of false doctrine and unbiblical teaching we point out in the classroom.

Without delving into a lengthy doctrinal statement here, let's just list a few things that matter with the gospel and must become essentials as we attempt to move and multiply the gospel forward.[2] Every believer should be able to say that "we believe the Bible to be the inspired, the only infallible, authoritative Word of God."[3] I was initially amazed in the beginning how little the typical African pastor we teach really understands about both the sufficiency and authority of Scripture. You know why? Because they are surrounded by false teachers who promote extrabiblical teaching like the "health and wealth" gospel; "healing" ministries which promise that if you give money in faith to a faith healer, your faith will result in the healing of your sick child or loved one; deliverance ministries which promise deliverance from demon possession or influence; and the list goes on.

The common denominator of all these so-called "ministries" is that they exploit the Scriptures and import meaning into the biblical text that is not there. The problem doesn't usually lie with our pastors falling in with false teaching but rather not being able to properly refute it! Consequently, because they cannot rest in the sufficiency of the Bible itself to supply what is really necessary for spiritual growth and ministry, they are essentially silenced by their own lack of training. Freedom from this bondage equals true power to them.

One of our Rwandan trainers Pastor F. commented:

> In Africa, there are many so-called Evangelical organizations which are constantly telling people on radio and television that God works through gifted men and women who *heal* and *perform miracles* but who completely

---

2. As adopted by the National Association of Evangelicals, "Statement of Faith."

3. National Association of Evangelicals, "Statement of Faith."

disregard the teaching of God's word. Because of my training, I believe the Bible gives us everything we really need, and I'm very thankful to know this powerful truth. (See Pastor F. M. R.'s full story at the end of this chapter.)

These remaining five doctrinal elements are not only vitally important but also help us form key teaching subjects among our fourteen theological courses in training nationals. These subjects are built around these key doctrinal areas:

> *We believe that there is one God eternally existent in three persons: Father, Son and Holy Spirit.*
>
> We believe in the deity of our Lord Jesus Christ, in his virgin birth, in his sinless life, in his miracles, in his vicarious and atoning death through his shed blood, in his bodily resurrection, in his ascension to the right hand of the Father, and in his personal return in power and glory.
>
> We believe that for the salvation of lost and sinful people, regeneration by the Holy Spirit is absolutely essential.
>
> We believe in the present ministry of the Holy Spirit by whose indwelling the Christian is enabled to live a godly life.
>
> We believe in the resurrection of both the saved and the lost; they that are saved unto the resurrection of life and they that are lost unto the resurrection of damnation. We believe in the spiritual unity of believers in our Lord Jesus Christ.[4]

Because there is such a proliferation of false doctrine in Africa, there cannot be a doctrinal looseness in terms of teaching content. Christian *inclusivism* must be checked at the door of doctrinal *fidelity*! Without that assurance, cardinal doctrines basic to Christianity are at risk of either diminishment or destruction.

We carefully and faithfully warn our students that there are two vital areas of doctrine which Evangelical believers must be cautious about in terms of church training. The first is what we

---

4. National Association of Evangelicals, "Statement of Faith." Emphasis added.

believe and teach about the *person of Jesus Christ*. Confusion about either the divinity and humanity of Christ are oftentimes areas of controversy not only among the Christian cults but also those influenced by them. Unless Jesus is both God and man at the same time, Jesus cannot be a legitimate Savior for mankind.

The second vital area is what we believe about *the work of Jesus Christ*. Christ's substitutionary sacrifice on the cross was completely and entirely sufficient to pay for the sin of the entire world. We are subsequently saved by God's grace alone by believing in Christ's payment personally.

I remember on one occasion I was preaching in East Africa to a large gathering of churches when my message was interrupted by a known demon-possessed woman. She had begun parading partially naked in front of the large crowd as I taught about the work that Jesus completed on the cross. Her disruption seemed to be timed to hinder me from making clear that Jesus' blood was the only means God had provided to entirely pay for our sins so any person could be saved from the penalty of their sin. The crowd that morning needed to know and understand that Christ had paid for their sin in full. They did not need to trust partially in their own good works but in Christ's work alone. Church leaders who are uncertain about matters like this need theological training in the Scriptures. Out of anything we could offer national leaders, this is what they want more than anything else. The woman I mentioned was pulled aside by members of leadership who had long been attempting to work with her so that those listening would not be distracted by her.

What happens when pastors are trained?
Listen to Pastor G. N.:

> I came to understand that the gospel is rooted in theology. Solid theology is needed and, in our country, you must go to the city to find good training. But with no money it is not accessible for most of us. The on-site modular training classes with GBTF are doing the impossible for us and also training us to pass it on as trainers ourselves. (See Pastor G. N.'s story at the end of this chapter.)

## CONTEMPORARY MISSIONS: TWO KEY QUESTIONS

Again, why should this be important as Westerners? Because many nationals haven't been sufficiently trained, they are ineffective with the gospel to adequately understand the doctrines which support it! We all know that false teaching abounds in the absence of sound doctrine. Having trained extensively in Africa for over thirteen years, I can assure you that every false idea that has ever come down the pike is taught on this continent! The reason for this is simple. National pastors outside the major cities in the rural areas don't have physical or financial access to theological training. Therefore, the vast majority of people are easy targets for various cults, pagan and animistic religions, along with the healing, deliverance, and health and wealth gospel movements. When false teachers come to these areas the people are easily influenced. Oftentimes, these very people will appear at the healing campaigns along with their sick family members.

As a result, I have personally witnessed thousands of people gather at a faith healer's compound on a weekend bringing their loved ones and all the money they could gather up to give to a healer in exchange for a grand healing experience. I have then watched the same people stumbling home late Sunday night bewildered and empty because they were told they didn't have sufficient faith for the healing of their family members. Those whose loved ones died en route or on-site were then held responsible to take the bodies off the ministry property and get them home in order to bury them. These are the sad but true realities of those under the oppressive nature of false doctrine and its purveyors.

We train nationals to understand that the whole gospel is accurate only if its doctrinal foundation is accurate. When someone in any culture knows how to properly communicate the gospel effectively within the context of their own culture with a heart like Jesus, people not only listen, they respond. For over thirteen years, Global Baptist Training Foundation has been doing just that: training nationals to reach their own nations with the gospel of Jesus Christ. The result? Exponential multiplication!

## Voices of the Nationals

Missionaries also need *practical training*.

In less than a decade, over 1,600 churches have been started by trained nationals, countless numbers of people brought to faith in Christ, and thousands baptized. In 2024 alone, the pastors GBTF trained started 455 new churches in Africa. By the end of the fourth quarter of the year our Western, Eastern, and Southern regional coordinators collected the data from the leadership of all 455 churches. The report was staggering. The collective data of all the churches showed that just over 50,000 souls had come to faith in Christ and the churches had already baptized the majority of them into the membership of these new church plants.

You say, "I've never heard of numbers like that in the context of Christian missions." Frankly, until the churches began to proliferate among our trained pastors, we hadn't either. Neither our staff, board, nor donors had any sense of what the results might be from training and empowering nationals. Once we began thinking in very practical terms of trained nationals starting new churches immediately upon being trained did we see the potential.

In fact, for nearly a seven-year period as GBTF steadily grew, all I did was travel and teach, travel and teach, rinse and repeat. I seldom looked up or considered slowing down as we walked through every door God opened into a new country. But then as God opened those doors, we began working hard at identifying not only potential leaders who would become regional coordinators and local trainers, but also church planters. Not only did we admonish and train every church leader in every class to go out and train ten others, but we began to sponsor new church planters funded by an organization that wanted to come alongside our efforts. The confidence behind this multiplication of trainers and church planters was the *practical training* they had received along with their academic training. What has happened since then has been truly phenomenal.

My prayer in this book is that the voices of the nationals will help lay out the case for training nationals as opposed to simply sending Western personnel at great costs accompanied by greatly reduced results. As I talked about in an earlier book entitled

## CONTEMPORARY MISSIONS: TWO KEY QUESTIONS

*Indigenous*,[5] we are not arguing against sending pioneer missionaries or teams unto unreached people groups who have never heard the gospel. The reality is that in the 10/40 window, we will have to employ pioneer methods to enter these cultures. Translation issues with the Scriptures will have to be conquered. Language, culture, and many other logistical problems will have to be solved. However, the one goal of the pioneer gospel agent is the same goal of training any other existing nationals. Nationals much be reached with the gospel and then trained to reach their own cultures and peoples with the gospel. The bottom line is to recognize that we must be ready to employ both pioneer and perpetuation methods! However, where there are indigenous believers in any locale, my prayer is that we would train them, equip them, and empower them through theological and practical training! The preparation the national receives is the key which unlocks the doors to extraordinary results among the indigenous. I think you'll agree, the nationals, as well as the results they produce, will speak for themselves.

## PASTOR N. R.

> If you can trust the African with the gospel of Christ, why can't you trust the African with the institutions of the gospel?

N. came to our classes in Entebbe, Uganda, and graduated in 2023. It was not until he became a trainer that I really understood the depth of his story. N. was born in Southwestern Uganda in what is known as the Ntungamo District. He was the twenty-seventh of thirty-two children in his father's household of sixteen wives. His father was a wealthy man by local standards because he owned a lot of land and hundreds of cows. He was also admittedly pagan and worshiped the spirits of his ancestors, who they considered to be gods. He somehow allowed N.'s birth mother to have his infant

---

5. Snavely, *Indigenous*, x, 15–17.

son sprinkled at the local Anglican church. N. proudly said that the interpretation of "N." means "lion."

Unfortunately, N.'s home life was highly chaotic, and he never had any memory of going to a church or hearing anything to do with the Bible. In fact, his father was never really committed to allowing his son to have any real chance at education or life beyond his chaotic home life. Primary school, which usually begins at five years of age, didn't happen for N. until he was ten. After completing three years of his primary school content in one year, N. found himself on the wrong side of his father's temper. Shortly thereafter his father threw him out of his house in a fit of rage, and the young ten-year-old was suddenly on his own. He lived in the bush for nearly a month. He never told me how he survived this ordeal, and I never asked, but he made it. Then a relative heard of his plight and found him a job many miles away keeping cattle for another large landowner. A year later, N.'s father had found out where he lived and sent one of his brothers to find him and bring him home.

Upon returning to the household, he was sent back to Primary 2 by his father, but N. refused, saying that he belonged in Primary 3. N. won the battle and finished in 2003, but his father ordered that N. should never attend another school. His father's wishes came true until we met this young man in 2019 in our GBTF classes. Just a year after he was refused further education by his father, both his mother and father died just days apart in 2004. At that time N. was isolated and on his own. He was unable to sustain himself in his home village, so he left and moved to Mbarara to find work. Young, bitter, and alone, N. began to drink and eventually became an alcoholic. While drunk, he would take his hostility out on others fistfighting. He was thrown in jail on multiple occasions. During this period of his life, he also became addicted to drugs.

While caught up in this hopeless cycle of self-destruction, N. viciously beat a man and the victim later reported him to the local police. When the police came to arrest him he resisted and attempted to escape. He was caught and charged with two serious offenses which would have likely kept him incarcerated for up

## CONTEMPORARY MISSIONS: TWO KEY QUESTIONS

to twenty years. N. said that while he was waiting for the vehicle which transports prisoners, the officer in charge of his interrogation asked him why he had beaten the man and resisted arrest. N. told him his story, and upon hearing his honest and forthright account of what happened, the officer whispered in his ear that he was going to give him a second chance. Immediately, the officer began to intimidate the complainant to force him to withdraw the charges. He also pressured the other police officers who dealt with N. resisting arrest to drop their charges against the young man. The plan was successful, and N. walked out of the precinct that night a free man. He had never known such mercy and questioned why this man fought so hard to become his advocate.

He couldn't fully understand why this unusual act of kindness had happened to him at this time. Personally, he hated God because the only association of God he knew was a God who could not have cared for him. He figured if a deity was in control but had allowed his life to be so out of control, he wanted nothing to do with this kind of God. But something else was taking place at nearly the same time N. had been spared from prison.

He had begun listening to an evangelical teacher at night on the local radio station in Mbarara who had captured his attention. This teacher was different, he said, because he actually encouraged his radio listeners to follow along with him with a Bible. So, N. borrowed a Bible from his neighbor and carefully listened to him to make sure he was actually teaching what he said the Scripture was saying. After some time, N. said one night the preacher encouraged those who wanted to become Christians to call upon the Lord to save them from eternal separation from God and come to a personal relationship with Jesus Christ. That night he gave his heart to Christ, and N. said from that moment forward, his life was completely and entirely changed.

One thing that haunted N. was his former communication and how his speech so dishonored God. He asked the Lord to help him use his formerly corrupted mouth to honor the Lord and help build other people up. From that simple prayer, God called N. to ministry and used him in a variety of ways beyond what he ever considered to be possible. His once-evil tongue has become a fountain of life in Mbarara and all over Uganda.

It wasn't long after N.'s graduation from the GBTF theological program that our leadership team asked N. to became a trainer in Southwestern Uganda for the foundation. He is now holding classes all over his region and continues to demonstrate a high level of both commitment and faithfulness to the cause of training nationals in his country. He agrees with the premise of GBTF based upon 2 Tim 2:1–7 that nationals are best suited for ministry in his country because they share the same language, culture, and love for the people, but he added that GBTF is unique among American-based organizations with which he was familiar. He says that GBTF stands out from all others "because they have truly and fearlessly decentralized their operations in order to put the nationals in control of the ministry. Unlike many mission organizations which have come and gone, GBTF has inverted the model to put the national in control."

In a written response to our interview questions regarding the impact that American missionaries had upon his area of Uganda, N. thoughtfully and passionately responded with his own question:

> If you can trust the African with the gospel of Christ, why can't you trust the African with the institutions of the gospel? That's why many churches, radio stations, Bible colleges, etc., started by missionaries cease operations 3–5 years after the missionaries leave. This lack of trust in African nationals with the institutions of the gospel has crippled the gospel in Africa. This is why GBTF is growing exponentially on the continent under trained African leadership.

Pastor N.'s story is one of many you will read in these pages, but perhaps no one has surprised our leadership both here and in Africa more than this individual. Recently, Pastor N. sent a model of an app which he created specifically for GBTF to be used organizationally to track theological classrooms, trainers' schedules, classroom results, new church plants started by trained nationals, and

CONTEMPORARY MISSIONS: TWO KEY QUESTIONS

the totality of evangelistic activity being accomplished by trained GBTF nationals across the continent. It has been recognized as an exceptional piece of work and will be fully implemented by the end of 2025. At the same time GBTF Africa will have a continent-wide website (created by N.) capable of receiving donations from fellow Africans in each country in which GBTF is registered. We are now working to make that happen as rapidly as possible.

Pastor N. is now the GBTF IT director for all of Africa. We trust the eternal impact of this man's ministry is just beginning in his native Uganda and throughout the continent! N.'s story is not only one of redemption but of how God has chosen to use nationals to exponentially multiply the gospel forward all over the world.

## PASTOR F. M. R.

> Africa's churches do not need the promise of miraculous signs to validate the gospel but theological training to accurately pass biblical truth on to other faithful men.

F. was born in the Congo just a few years after Belgium granted independence to the DRC in 1960. F. was the oldest of his other eleven brothers and sisters. Both of his parents were believers, and he was fortunate to grow up in a godly home where he could have access to the teachings of Scripture. He was taught to read by learning the Bible from his mother and father at home, came to know Christ before ten years of age, and was baptized in the river adjacent to the church.

F. says that his earliest memories include his reading the Bible on his own and having a period of fasting one day each week to pray and seek the Lord's will for his life. He continues this practice today and believes it to be the cornerstone of his growth and maturity in Christ over a lifetime of Christian service. He is one of the few believers I know anywhere in the world who fasts on a regular basis and credits the practice to his deep walk with the Lord. In the course of his spiritual walk, F. has read through the word of God at least six times verse by verse.

## Voices of the Nationals

In 1998, at the onset of civil war, he, along with the rest of his entire church, were rounded up by Congolese rebels on Saturday, August 15, and locked inside the building of the church in which he had grown up. His captors told them that on Tuesday, August 18, the church would be set on fire, and they would watch and laugh at them as they perished in the flames. One of their captors mocked them by throwing a Bible inside the window, shouting, "Let's see if God will save you as you burn like the wood of this building."

F. said that in the midst of their impending doom, he never believed that God would allow them to burn to death. He told his other captives that he knew God had promised to use him, and so they would not die. Instead, he, along with the other pastors, read the Scriptures their captors had thrown at them, gaining comfort and claiming the promises of God's power to protect them. All of Sunday and Monday, the rebels stacked wood around the building.

By Tuesday midday, before the rebels could start the fire, four local men attacked the rebels, killing several of them. Of the scores of people locked in the church, and of those who freed them, only four people perished that day. God truly answered F.'s prayer, confirming God's promise to him and the church members.

In 2012, nearly fourteen years after this incident in the Congo and eighteen years after the Rwandan genocide, we had the opportunity of offering the training to F. and fifty-four other men who had been handpicked to replace those pastors slaughtered in the genocide of 1994. Although faithful in their ministries to keep their churches going after replacing their slain pastors, their lack of training was extremely apparent. Reading the Scripture was often the extent of what many of them could offer their congregations. Year by year, we returned to teach these men one theological course after another. Finally, in 2020, we were able to hold the official graduation of this Rwandan classroom. It was truly a milestone in the lives of these brave men and has proven to be a model respected by the government of Rwanda. Paul Kagame, Rwandan president, instituted an austere program whereby church pastors who could not demonstrate that they had "official" theological training would not be able to pastor Rwandan churches. When the policy was

## CONTEMPORARY MISSIONS: TWO KEY QUESTIONS

instituted in 2024, all GBTF graduates were able to remain in their churches and ministries because the government recognized the theological program of GBTF as a valid theological school.

Let me allow Pastor F. M. R. to finish his story:

> One of the reasons I think GBTF has been so successful here in Rwanda and all over Africa is because they respect us as Africans. They did not come here to make us like them in the way we dress or in the way we eat. They came to equip us through the training. Africa's churches do not need the promise of miraculous signs to validate the gospel but theological training so we can pass biblical truth on to other faithful men. We are now empowered by our learning because we know that knowledge is power.

## PASTOR G. N.

> I came to understand that the gospel is rooted in theology. Theology must be learned, and in our country you must go to the city to find good training. But with no money it is not accessible for most of us.

Pastor G. was born in the Kayanza Province of Burundi in 1978. His family went to the local Catholic church in their village and were known as those who both brewed and drank banana beer. Since bananas were plentiful, they had little trouble either making it, selling it, or using it. Pastor G. said they did all of these. However, as G. grew up, his parents wanted him to go to school for his education and hopefully grow up to be different from them. Had his family worshiped pagan deities or been involved in traditional religions, this would never have taken place. Unfortunately, G. said he didn't respect his parents, and he made little effort to do anything well.

In 1994, G. heard the gospel through an evangelical ministry that had come to his village. For the first time in his life G. understood the gospel, and he gave his heart and life to Jesus Christ. He continued his education at the local secondary school in his town.

One day at school a preacher spoke to the students about Christianity and serving God with their lives and talents. He decided to surrender to God's calling in his life to serve God in the church. The church where he was baptized as a new believer had a Bible institute which trained new pastors and deacons for church service. After he finished secondary school, he completed his studies at the Bible institute and was immediately called in 2007 to become the pastor of a church in a much larger city from where he grew up and went to school as a young man. It was here he met his wife and started his young family.

While he was the pastor of this small church, his wife worked to help him earn his university degree in community development. It had been his dream to be able to go to university, and he said not long after he finished his work for his degree, another dream was fulfilled in his life. This took place in 2021 when the GBTF Rwandan Coordinator came to his town to hold the first GBTF training class in theology. Pastor G. had received a lot of practical help from his Bible institute in 2007, but he now began to understand the value of theological education in his life and ministry. After finishing the fourteen courses of subject material, G. was invited by the GBTF staff to coordinate training classrooms in his own country under the leadership of native Burundians.

Today, as one of the leading trainers in Burundi, Pastor G. N. says:

> I came to understand that the gospel is rooted in theology. Theology must be learned and, in our country, you must go to the city to find good training. But with no money, it is inaccessible for most of us. The on-site modular training classes GBTF offers are doing the impossible for us and also training us to pass it on as trainers ourselves.

However, these indigenous believers are not only passing on what they learn by training others in their own regions, they also spread the word to those outside of their countries. As I shared earlier, we have never once picked up a phone to contact nationals about training them. Just the opposite is true. They hear about

## CONTEMPORARY MISSIONS: TWO KEY QUESTIONS

a classroom sometimes hundreds of miles from their village in a bordering country and contact the local host of that classroom. I have lost track of the number of times this has happened over the years. God is allowing us to open six new countries each year through this exact process!

# CHAPTER FOUR

## Why Train the Nationals?

LET'S PIVOT FOR FEW moments to reflect on why evangelical leaders should be focused on training the nationals to reach their own nations for Christ.

Frankly, Christians have been doing mission work a long time since the Savior charged the first disciples to spread the gospel. Fast-forwarding to our own continent, for the last 250 years, American evangelicals have made a significant impact in pioneering the gospel message to nearly every continent. Due to these pioneer efforts, there are multiplied numbers of Bible translations in hundreds of languages and dialects around the globe making the word of God available. Consequently, there are existing believers in many countries of the world who do not require pioneer mission efforts. What is needed is a strategy for identifying believers in places like this who can in turn be trained and empowered for ministry.

I must confess that, for many years as a church planter, I did not understand this concept found in Paul's final Epistle to Timothy and the world. I thought that if I started a church on the field where God had directed me, that I should pastor that church indefinitely. Even when moving on from that church plant, I made sure they had "competent" leadership by searching out another American "missionary" who could assume leadership. I simply did

## WHY TRAIN THE NATIONALS?

not think in terms of training nationals to do what I was doing. Why not? For one thing, I hadn't been trained that way myself. I had drunk the Kool-Aid of American superiority in resources, training, and abilities. I was taught only the model of the pioneer missionary.

Nonetheless, I was not a pioneer in any of the places God had directed me to plant a church. There were other believers, although small in number, present on the ground. My audience also spoke my language, had access to good Bibles, lived on the same socioeconomic level, and had many cultural similarities. All that being said, I never sat down and prayed about training future pastors in my own church plants to essentially take over my job! Fortunately, this is not true everywhere on the missions spectrum. Many Western mission pastors actively begin a process whereby they will replace themselves with a national pastor once they have successfully launched a church plant. Unfortunately, this has not always been the case in mission organizations.

The problem in many mission churches started by American missionaries is the transition to the national pastor groomed by the Western pastor. Once the Western missionary is gone, the church will often struggle under its national pastor. It is not necessarily because the pastor is *unable* to fill the position; it is because he may never *measure up* to the founding pastor in the eyes of the nationals themselves. Churches like this will often fail or split within 3–5 years of the founding pastor's departure.

Another issue arises when the American organizations retain ownership of the church land and buildings. This is widespread, and, as I have learned from the nationals, it creates a great divide that both discourages and confuses the nationals.

We have monitored the church planters and their churches for the past decade in regard to their long-term health, and the results are shocking. With over 1,600 churches started in the last ten years by GBTF, less than ten church-starts have failed completely. I think the reason for this points directly to the training of the pastors. It also demonstrates that local pastors who know the language, understand the culture, and care deeply about their

## Voices of the Nationals

people anchor the church more successfully than anyone else on the planet! This is not unusual! In fact, being reminded of Paul's admonition to Timothy about reproducing leaders on the ground (as Titus had been commanded to do in Crete) strongly suggests this to be integral to Missions 101. After all, if Paul had both commanded this principle as well as practiced it, why don't our basic missions models reflect it more explicitly?

I shared in my book *Indigenous*, written about eight years after this ministry began, that I thought that I would need to find nationals to train through Western missionaries already on the field. What I soon discovered was that most missionaries were not nearly as focused on providing theological training to nationals as I thought, and secondly, I found that national pastors and church leaders were actually looking and praying for organizations who could come and train them! However, their need and desire for proper training must coincide with access to training. These groups hear about our work through GBTF and reach out. We have never had to contact anyone. We do have a vetting process, but, basically, our work self-propagates; so strong is the desire of nationals to get solid, biblical theological training.

Pastor J. T. reported:

> After many years of praying for an open door for nationals to get theological training, it has finally arrived through Global Baptist Training Foundation. Our pastors could never afford or have access to expensive Bible college or seminary training. GBTF is vitally changing the spiritual landscape of Liberia and all of the African continent.
> (See Pastor J. T.'s story at the end of this chapter.)

So, when we can provide mobile classrooms relatively near their locations, they make every conceivable effort to come to the training. Another pastor who never had access to training or the ability to pay for it said:

> Nationals who can learn theology where they live is a great blessing. This method of local classrooms allows all our pastors to gather and learn together not far from

## WHY TRAIN THE NATIONALS?

home and yet still be able to get the finest learning materials we have ever known. My vision for the future is to reproduce this training with others just like I have received myself!
(See Pastor D. M.'s story at the end of this chapter.)

I remember on one teaching occasion in Togo, we were given permission to hold our classroom at an old evangelical seminary in the capitol city. We had about sixty students, and the class was faithfully attended for over three years. The interesting thing was that during our "free" class to all of these pastors who normally could not afford to pay for seminary education, the seminary was holding classes for students who could pay for their studies. The class had five students! (Even if many of these national pastors had funding for training, uprooting and moving to a large center for training is practically impossible. Most are bivocational, with farming being the number-one occupation, and they have families and churches depending on them!)

One of our particular organization's with a few exceptions, is that we will not hold a classroom anywhere that cannot produce a minimum of thirty students. Most of the classrooms have not less than fifty and as many as 120! Consequently, I have never had to make that first call to a Western missionary or missions organization in order to facilitate making connections with national pastors. So how does a national training organization locate its students? Not a full month had passed after our decision to step out on faith and begin this training ministry when, in February, a Burmese pastor visiting the US walked by my office with a pastor friend of mine. When he heard about what I was doing, he excitedly returned to my office to find out more about what God was leading us to do. I cannot describe the joy that came over that pastor's face when he understood our vision for training nationals. He said this was the answer to many years of prayer. (Myanmar [Burma] has been through a series of coups and military takeovers. The country is simply not safe most of the time. When GBTF first began, one of our rationales was that in the future, the day could come when we couldn't get into many nations of the world. We have seen that in real time in countries like Myanmar, Haiti, and Congo. Fortunately, we had trained so many pastors in these countries that, in most cases, the training continues through nationals. We often fund this training, but the nationals are doing it.)

Pastor S., of Togo, said, "We have been praying for someone like you to come and now we finally know who you are."

Within the next year, I would be teaching a group of about thirty Burmese pastors a course in biblical interpretation. I was actually teaching a group of fifth-generation Christians who traced their spiritual lineage to my spiritual hero, Adoniram Judson, the first missionary to leave the shores of America in 1812.

I also had a Congolese student at a Bible college here in the US. When he found out about our starting GBTF, he called the leader of a Baptist group of pastors in Kigali, Rwanda. By the middle of 2012, I was teaching a large group of men who had replaced those pastors massacred in the Rwandan genocide. The leader of this courageous group of men told me:

> When this training ministry came to us, it was a miracle to me because at the time we needed someone to help us who had the ability to teach theology from the Scriptures. I feel that God brought the answer to our prayers.
> (See Pastor D. R.'s story at the end of this chapter)

At the same time, God opened the door to a large group of pastors in the central-western region of the Congo just across the border. Time and again our website was discovered by nationals who desired theological training. Sometimes our office phone would ring with an African national on the other end asking for our classes to be taught in their country. On more than one occasion these individuals who called became the host pastors in their respective countries for a new GBTF classroom. New countries opened to GBTF are usually adjacent to the border of the country in which we are presently teaching. On nearly every occasion, when we felt it was time to move into a new country, we would discover that at least one or two of our student pastors had crossed a border to come to the existing classroom. This would lead to conversations regarding when we would show up in their own country with these

## WHY TRAIN THE NATIONALS?

pastors acting as our hosts or knowing those who could become hosts.

Most of the time, the vast majority of these individuals, or those they represent in either East Asia or in Central Africa, had never had solid theological training of any kind. They all said that Bible college and seminary training was only in the urban areas, and it was neither accessible nor affordable. Many of these men and women who attended our classes were from the bush areas or jungle villages. Over the years of training national pastors, I have discovered four highly significant things that demonstrate why they are so deeply effective at reaching their populations with the gospel.

*First*, nationals in Africa and around the world are not necessarily looking for a free handout from American missionaries or international organizations. Will they take it if it is offered? Yes, they will, but it is not the primary thing they really want or deeply desire. For decades we have interviewed our students to know how to best provide for them. What we have discovered is that if money, resources, or theological training are offered, they want training. You know why? They instinctively know that training involves knowledge and knowledge translates into power! This is why they will slog for hours over the washed-out roads and pay such a high personal price just to get to a teaching site. This is why they will sleep on a concrete floor 4–5 nights in a row. This is why they will save their resources for months to provide their own travel and food expenses once they have arrived!

Therefore, they not only want the same training available to most Western people in ministry, but they are also willing to make significant sacrifice in order to obtain it. They understand that money and resources are short-lived assets, but training can be leveraged for the kingdom of God indefinitely! They of course, are absolutely right. (We have had national pastors sell computers, work extra fields, etc., to raise funding to get to our GBTF teaching sites.)

*Secondly*, the indigenous believers need to have skin in the game of receiving free theological training. They must be reminded that they are receiving a first-rate theological training program. It is being brought to their country and region and provided through trained men of God who, through other people of God, have sacrificed greatly to make it available to them. The written resources are given to them in their native tongue and taught personally in a modular format.

Therefore, students are notified by our regional representatives of the class no less than ninety days in advance. This gives them time to save their own resources for travel to the teaching site and set aside money for food to eat while they are in class, along with purchasing a syllabus in the local dialect covering the subject matter being taught. When the students are taught to sacrifice to get access to the training, they are able to take full ownership because they have some real skin in the game, too!

*Thirdly*, indigenous believers in Christ need to have ownership of their own local ministries. For decades many Western missionaries have left Christian believers on mission fields all over the world woefully unprepared to carry on the work of Jesus Christ *confidently*. Therefore, the results of much of our mission efforts have not produced the long-term fruit expected. In most cases, I do not believe most Western missionaries had intentions of hurting but rather of helping the cause of Christ. Unfortunately, that didn't always happen.

For several years, I have been privy to conversations held by national pastors I was training regarding their life experiences with Western missionaries. The complaints and deep-seated frustrations of these national pastors greatly surprised me and, in many cases, shocked me to the core. I heard story after story of Western missionary families who maintained social and spiritual distances from the very people they had supposedly come to love with the gospel, lead to Christ, and then train for future ministry. Instead of leaving a legacy of training, life example, and ministry for nationals to emulate and sustain, the churches, ministries, radio stations, orphanages, etc., Western missionaries had begun would greatly diminish or fail within five years of their departure. Why?

Because, in most cases, the nationals were ill-equipped to manage them. They had, in many ways, been taught, either directly or indirectly, to depend on the resources of the missionary rather than themselves within their own cultural context. However, because we do not operate like many NGOs that do a lot of giving but demand little, we take considerable time in training nationals in how God sees them as perfect equals with anyone else in the world, particularly Westerners. If they have had considerable experience working alongside Western missionaries, this is unfortunately, in many cases, not how they have historically viewed themselves.

## WHAT HAPPENS WHEN NATIONALS ARE TRAINED?

Several key things happen when nationals are trained to take complete ownership of their own ministries. First, a national's ownership of ministry is grounded in knowing that God is no respecter of persons ethnically, racially, or socially. After training in Africa for several months I began to see a pattern developing regarding the national's perception of themselves in relation to both American and European ministry groups whom they had either worked alongside or under. I noticed that they almost always saw their mentor groups as possessing greater access to ministry supplies and even to God's blessings than they did themselves as nationals. Over time, I came to the conclusion that without direct intervention and teaching, this cycle would never be broken. I knew I was going to have to change the way I presented our foundation, but also how I presented the God we mutually served.

In classroom after classroom, I began to essentially lecture my fellow African pastors about who they were in Christ, about how the God they served was the same God I served, and that He was not only no respecter of persons, but that He was ready to provide for them exactly as He had always provided for me. After every such session, I saw a multitude of different reactions. For some, they stood to their feet and praised God while others fell to their knees and wept tears of joy. Since that time, I have seen how these same pastors and church leaders have begun to act toward me and the mutual respect that has replaced their lack of identity.

Secondly, nationals who "own it" take their personal preparation seriously. The vast majority of the indigenous value their own training for ministry more than anything else not available to them normally. In the classroom they are serious, sensible listeners, and sensitive to theological truth rooted in Scripture. Even though they have the course materials in front of them, they almost always take copious notes so as not to forget an illustration or point that I might add. It has always been difficult over the years to hold back questions during a day of training.

One of the great issues we face with them is proliferation of false doctrine related to the apostolic period. Deliverance ministries, prophetic ministries, and healing ministries, each centered around a self-proclaimed teacher, often misapply the sign gifts and require careful study and proper application for the students. However, once the national pastor or student is trained, they normally do not reenter that world again. Theologically prepared, indigenous pastors, deacons, and evangelists enter ministry vigorously, determined to apply their preparation seriously once empowered by the truth!

The indigenous pastor can also be greatly impacted by training received in just one class. For instance, in the systematic study of salvation called *soteriology*, the subject includes a section on the eternal security of the believer in Christ. Because many of our national pastors have never had a fully orbed study on salvation, they have not understood this related doctrine sufficiently. However, once they are taught, their ministries are revolutionized by just this one area of theological study.

A similar impact was noticed when we taught pastoral leadership and church administration in a country recently opened to GBTF. In a break during the morning session, two or three pastors approached the trainer (a national trainer) in tears asking for God's forgiveness because they realized that they had not led their churches in a biblical or godly manner. The result? That week was a period of widespread revival among scores of pastors gathered for that particular class.

Pastor T. N. responded:

> The first change we saw is that men, women, and young people in our churches have come and repented of their hidden wrongs. These ungodly practices had been going on for many years. Following the differences made in our congregations, we began to see new church plants being started by newly committed pastors. New villages that had not been evangelized now had churches starting in them. Many people were being saved and baptized, and we were rejoicing at what God was doing through us.
> (See Pastor T. N.'s story at the end of this chapter.)

Thirdly, nationals have the intangible element of cultural toughness. We typically call this an indomitable spirit. In Africa, for instance, they simply do not flinch at challenge or danger in the same way most Westerners do. This is clearly part of their identity as a people group who have had to survive very difficult life circumstances on an almost daily basis. Consequently, when situations arise where most of us might throw in the towel, they simply find another way to succeed.

One of our trainers, Pastor J., who we helped escape an unjust arrest and possible death in a state marked by civil war, made the decision to go back in to teach a class he had committed to months before without notifying us of his decision. (We would have strongly urged him not to do so.) After the class was over and he had safely returned to the safe house we had provided for him and his family, we asked him why he endangered himself, because in our eyes it appeared reckless and unnecessary.

This was his response:

> I had to take the risk because there were sixty-seven students who were gathered and committed to this class which was scheduled since January. I told myself not to disappoint these learners who were eager to learn. There was no other trainer available. [One of his students was his father who had been in ministry since he was eighteen yet without any training.]
> (See Pastor J. K.'s story at the end of this chapter)

## Voices of the Nationals

But, there is also the physical and emotional toughness which all of our trainers exemplify. Pastor S., who is a trainer in a closed country, was recently returning home from teaching a class in a larger city north of his home. Not long before reaching his house, his team was stopped by a rebel group. They were stripped and robbed of their money and phones. Fortunately, he had placed his remaining cash in the pages of his Bible. When asked by the rebels why he carried a Bible, he replied that he was a pastor. For whatever reason, his captors showed respect to him and never examined his Bible. He made it home with his cash but without his GBTF-provided iPhone 8!

Safety is simply not something that many nationals have any guarantees of in their daily lives. They begin and end each day knowing that life is hard, and they must be willing to fight through their battles in order to succeed. Last year, during rainy season, G. U. O., one of our toughest trainers, took a bus to a particular teaching site north of where he lived, but the bus got hopelessly stuck in the mud. Consequently, G. U. O. was forced to take a motorcycle taxi for several remaining miles. A few miles from his destination, the motorbike also got swamped in the mud and could not continue. G. U. O. was forced to pull on his boots and walk the remaining few miles. He trudged on in his knee-length rubber boots and opened the class. Most Westerners would have simply waited for the dry season.

G. U. O. humbly says:

> As a national it is easy for us to reach certain areas which might be hard for a foreigner. When I go to some districts, I sleep on the dusty floor of a grass thatched hut. There is no hotel one can use, but, as a national, I can adjust to such a situation.
> (See G. N.'s story in chapter 4.)

Finally, when nationals take ownership of their own ministries, they become independent versus dependent. Unfortunately, most American mission agencies have not done well in developing nationals to become totally independent of their American

## WHY TRAIN THE NATIONALS?

mentors. Over the last thirteen years, I have heard repeatedly from nationals all over the African continent who have confided their true feelings about Western mission agencies. They have consistently said that, in one way or another, their mentors failed to invest in them sufficiently in order to take over their ministries and prosper as indigenous believers after the missionaries were gone. More often than not, churches, physical structures, and long-term investments did not survive the test of time.

Let's be honest, some of this is to be expected. However, in many cases, the Western, often American, missionaries and their agencies sought to build their own kingdoms that could not survive after they picked up and moved on. Listen to what one national leader named Pastor N. said to me over breakfast one morning:

> Many American mission organizations struggle to relinquish control of ministry to national pastors, fearing that they may not grasp their vision or ministry perspective. However, if American missionaries can trust the indigenous leaders with the gospel, why can't they trust them with the institutions which ultimately support the gospel?
> (See Pastor N.'s story at the end of this chapter.)

It's not that the nationals couldn't lead them, manage them, or see God prosper them. It was rather the lack of spiritual, theological, and personal training necessary to confidently perpetuate them forward into the next generation. This has been the predominant testimony I have heard for well over a decade of training nationals around the world, particularly on the African continent.

If our essential hope in Christ's promised return to earth as King is predicated on complete world evangelization, we must commit ourselves to reaching our world through the training and empowering of the nationals. The indigenous instinctively know the language systems, the cultures in which they live, and can usually navigate them freely in the growing number of nations closed to most Westerners. We can be certain that as we continue to move into cultures more hostile to the gospel, particularly in the 10/40 window nations, we will see a determined effort to prevent access to Western influencers. How this will take shape is different in each culture and political environment. However, in each case, the training, equipping, and enabling of the nationals on the ground is both the biblical and essential method for moving and multiplying the gospel forward. I believe the time is now to both train them and explicitly trust them with the gospel of Jesus Christ within their cultures.

## PASTOR D. R.

> I told my wife and my kids to not be afraid because God told me that we will not die and we will stand before King Jesus. That was the promise I got from God.

D. R. is someone you could not forget once you meet him in person. If you ever wondered what it might be like to meet an African chief in person, you're getting close to what it is like to know D. I first met him in July of 2012. I was in Kigali, Rwanda, at his invitation to come teach a group of pastors who he himself had installed as pastors to replace those killed in the genocide eighteen years earlier. For me it was a strangely wonderful experience because I had never imagined myself being so involved with a group of men who had walked through what these men had experienced. They were not only walking survivors, but they were also desperately trying to serve the same God I personally knew. The similarities almost stopped there because they, unlike me, had never known the educational opportunities I had been given.

For many of them, reading the Scripture to their congregations on Sunday mornings and praying was literally the extent of what they had to offer them. Their understanding of how to exegete the text of Scripture for their congregations, sometimes quite large, was simply not possible for them. Of course, I knew little of this when I first stood before them for our initial class in hermeneutics that July of 2012. Not long after opening this first class I was soon to learn not only about them primarily as genocide survivors but also how they perceived their mentor D. R. For them,

## WHY TRAIN THE NATIONALS?

D. was not only a leader but a living miracle who had appeared almost as an angel in the immediate aftermath of the Rwandan nightmare between April and July of 1994.

In those initial days after the cessation of murder and mayhem, D. walked over countless corpses in order to discover who remained of the Tutsi and sympathetic Hutu populations all over the tiny country of Rwanda. He, too, was a survivor of the three-month holocaust. The morning it began, Hutu killers came to his house to kill him and his family. He said at that moment he was sitting in his living room, and he started to pray. The attackers heard gunshots outside and turned and ran, taking their machetes with them. But, they came back. Two weeks later, they returned to kill D. who was at the top of their list of those they wanted dead.

But, this second time, D. said the killers walked into his living room. He was in the same chair, his family hidden in a closet as before. D. said the men who had come to kill him looked bewildered, almost like they might be in the wrong house. That turned to fear and then to abject terror on their faces as they turned and ran away, never to return. D. said that he believes they encountered angels better armed than they were!

He said, "And then I got the answers from God and I told my wife and my kids to not be afraid because God told me that we will not die and we will stand before King Jesus. That was the promise I got from God."

D. later said that God had answered his prayer during the genocide that no one in his family would be killed. It was now eighteen years later and here I was sitting in the midst of nearly sixty men who owed their present ministry callings to this man they revered as their fearless leader. D. sat in nearly every class and listened intently as I poured into these brave men of God year after year.

After the Rwanda men and women graduated D. reflected:

> When this training ministry came to us it was a miracle to me because at the time we needed someone to help us who had the ability to teach theology from the Scriptures. I feel that God brought the answer to our prayers

because Dr. Bruce came and faithfully taught our pastors for nearly a decade. Year after year their skills have significantly improved.

What D. didn't understand was that I was learning as much as my students in ways beyond theology and instructions on how to deliver a sermon. I was beginning a journey of faith that would lead me to see the incredible abilities of nationals to change their own worlds through training that would in turn produce intentional multiplication. Now nearly thirteen years later, the evidence of those early days is accumulating faster than I could have ever then imagined.

## PASTOR T. N.

> With this teaching from the Scriptures, we knew that we could never be the same again. We could never go back to our pulpits and act like nothing happened here. No, we were now understanding that a change had come that made us change, too. We have had a new beginning of ministry that has shown us how to honor God in all we do for Him.

Pastor T. N. was born in the Western Province Rutsiro District. By his own testimony he was born into a pagan family who practiced the traditional religion. His father made wooden idols and related worship objects which he used to abuse and overpower his family members. T. N. said this was also accompanied by his father being an alcoholic. Fortunately for T. N., his uncle understood his family's situation and prayed for T. N. He said that without the intervention of his uncle he doesn't know how he could have ever escaped the chaos and idolatry or his father's influence.

However, his father had seen the intervention of the uncle into T. N.'s life and wanted to stop T. N. from leaving his pagan roots, and so he attempted to poison him to death. A deacon from his uncle's church came to the home to pray for T. N., and T. N. survived the ordeal. After T. N. was recovered the deacon told him that God could deliver him from his alcohol addiction if he wanted to be free from it and its connections to pagan life. This was what T. N. really wanted, but he also knew that if he stopped his use of alcohol he would be abandoned by his entire family. Finally, he gathered the courage to tell his family, and, soon thereafter, he came to know Christ as his Savior. From the time of his poisoning to his conversion eight months had passed, but now he was free to serve God.

In 2011, T. N. was ordained to the gospel ministry. He served for many years without any formal training, but finally in 2023-24, T. N. finished all his courses from Global Baptist Training Foundation, and in February of 2024, he graduated with his diploma.

Before he had the opportunity to study with GBTF T. N. said:

> We had a big gap in our thinking regarding evangelism. Very few pastors, church leaders, and evangelists had ever had any training in church administration and church evangelism.

When our African director (Fidele Shinga) taught the first class in Western Rwanda, several of the pastors were so convicted about their lack of evangelism among their churches that they collectively wept when hearing what the Scriptures taught about sharing our faith with others.

> I remember when our GBTF trainers began to teach our pastors about evangelism, church planting, and church administration, we heard things for the first time that shook us to our roots. We wept and rejoiced before God that we were able to both hear the truth and then make the truth our practice.

The first changes reported to us from our leadership in Western Rwanda was that men, women, and young people in the churches were coming and repenting of their hidden wrongs. Some ungodly practices had been going on for many years. Following the differences made in the congregations, they began to see new church plants being started by newly committed pastors. New villages that had not been evangelized had churches starting in them. Many people were being saved, and Rwandan leaders were rejoicing at what God was doing through them because of their new training. T. N. states with renewed confidence:

> Our training has empowered us and taught us that our God is the same God and Father to us as the Western missionary. We can solve our own problems, and our faith has enlarged to know that God can supply all our needs without depending on anyone but God. This is our nation, and as citizens who are believers in Christ, we know that God has called us to reach our nation for him with the resources that He provides us. With this teaching from the Scriptures we knew that we could never be the same again. We could never go back to our pulpits and act like nothing happened here. No, we were now understanding that a change had come that made us change too. We have had a new beginning of ministry that has shown us how to honor God in all we do for Him.

## PASTOR K. J.

> That day, and that moment of speaking for the other students and myself, I found the fulfillment I had long sought in becoming a teacher of the word of God.

Pastor J. was born into a pastor's home on June 10, 1990, in the village of Kabushwa which borders on the nearby Biega National Park in the Democratic Republic of the Congo. J.'s early life was difficult. Because of their location, J.'s family lived under constant threat of looting, rape, and murder at the hands of the Hutu extremists who fled Rwanda after the end of the Rwandan genocide in 1994.

Despite the tough situation J. was able to attend school and church in the village where he lived. His parents always had high hopes for J., but the difficult traumatic days of the post-genocide era left J. confused and somewhat resistant to God's moving in his life. Even though he had come to know the Lord at this time, he did not have a heart to serve. By 2011 J. had finished all of his primary education and in 2011 began working toward his bachelor's degree

## WHY TRAIN THE NATIONALS?

in Bukavu, about sixty-five miles from his home. Because of the distance he had to board near the school while he was studying. Being away from his family was not easy for him at the time, but he knew that this educational opportunity would not last forever.

After several difficult years of starting, stopping, and starting again because of finances, he was able to graduate with honors in 2016. He was soon hired by a commercial company in 2017 in computer science and was also in charge of human resources. He then started his own company in 2018 and soon had over fifty employees before the bottom fell out of his life once again. During this time, J. reported that he had no time to go to church or take part in any worship on Sunday. Whatever time he had after work he spent on himself. He didn't realize that God not only couldn't but wouldn't bless his life while deliberately living for his own purposes.

In March of 2019, J. began attending church regularly once again, and in July he met and decided to marry one of the young ladies who was a faithful and committed member. J. had yet to know what it was that God wanted him to do. He had only recently opened his heart to that possibility once again. After marrying, J. and his young bride continued to attend church faithfully and to grow both in their relationship with each other and with God.

Despite his former hardness of heart and ingratitude toward God, J.'s father had always written to him and encouraged him towards spiritual things, reminding him that it was impossible to have anything in the world without it being God's will. He said, "Serve God with all your strength, and you'll see who He is for you and your future family."

By November of 2019, both J. and his wife had begun prayer and Bible study lessons with their pastor and had started to consider the idea of serving God with both their lives. A few weeks later they had a surprise visit with J.'s parents in the village to tell them about what God was doing in their hearts. His dad was filled with joy and fervently prayed for them before they left to go back home. Upon leaving he gave J. two Bibles and two commentaries about the Scriptures. This only fueled J.'s passion for spiritual things, and, a few weeks later, he was asked to conduct the services at his home church by the pastor. It was then that he recognized his call to ministry and submitted himself to God's will, whatever that may be. Continuing in their local church, serving in multiple capacities for the next few years, J. and his wife were also blessed with two boys during this time.

In December of 2021, J.'s father contacted him about a theological training course being offered in a church near his dad through Global Baptist Training Foundation. The class had sixty pastors present and J. attended the class knowing only one other pastor among them all. At the end of the week of classes J. was chosen to stand and give thanks for all the students to the GBTF trainer who had taught the course. He spoke of the occasion glowingly:

> That day, and that moment of speaking for the other students and myself, I found the fulfillment I had long sought in becoming a teacher of the word of God.

Since 2021, J. has finished his GBTF coursework and begun holding new classrooms in the Congo. Recently, we have made him the countrywide coordinator, and this was followed by a recent classroom being held in the capitol of Kinshasa. We sent J. there in August of 2024 during a time of sporadic rebel action both in the bush and in the capitol. Little did we know that because of J.'s contact with our leader in Rwanda and the large group of men that gathered for a GBTF class each day, the government would suspect him of having rebel connections with the Tutsi people in the DRC. This led to a wanted poster being placed in the capitol just days after he was to travel to hold classes on the other side of the country in Goma. However, his morning flight was canceled because the Goma airport had been taken over by rebels the previous night, and J. was unable to reuse his ticket. Within hours, we purchased another ticket for him to fly to Kigali and then come back into the Congo from the eastern border to retrieve his family. They were extricated back over the border by car the following day just hours before authorities came to arrest him.

## WHY TRAIN THE NATIONALS?

We rented a safe house in Rwanda for J. and his family while we waited for the Congo situation to settle down. While we were waiting for clarity concerning J.'s future for possibly returning home, J. failed to tell us that he had scheduled a GBTF classroom near his hometown of Bukavu in the southeastern region long before the rebel activity had escalated. Instead of notifying the local host that his situation would not allow him to teach the classroom, J. snuck back over the border to keep his commitment to the host and gathered students. We didn't know this until the class had finished and J. was safely back over the border in Rwanda. When asked why he had taken such a foolish risk (in our eyes) J. responded by saying:

> They had been waiting for this class for weeks and among the students was my own biological father. He has served the Lord since he was fifteen years of age and had never had an opportunity for training like this. I couldn't let the students down and disappoint them.

J. is now back in the Congo teaching nationals through GBTF. The political situation there still makes life very difficult, but J. and others continue to serve the Lord faithfully. Near where J. is, another Pastor, S., had a bomb drop onto his house as a result of the rebel war against the government. His wife and all five children were injured. GBTF was able to assist in their medical bills and helping them in the aftermath of this traumatic situation. They still suffer emotionally and have trouble sleeping as the bomb fell during the night. J. and S. are amazing examples of how nationals are on-site doing what would be virtually impossible for a Westerner.

## PASTOR G. U. O.

> When I go to some districts I sleep on the dusty floor of a grass thatched hut. There is no hotel one can use, but, as a national, I can adjust to any such situation.

G. U. O. was born in the Ndaro Village in the West Nile region of Uganda. His family were members of the Uganda Anglican

Church, and he played in the church youth band. He firmly believed that, on the basis of his infant baptism and confirmation as a teenager, he was undoubtedly heaven-bound. One evening the chairman of the band told Gilbert: "Young man, your service to God is vain without Christ." He said he was instantly convicted and, on that day, March 28, 1989, he received Jesus Christ by faith as his Savior. He told others, "I became a child of God and things changed for me." After finishing school in his home village, he met and eventually married the love of his life. G. said it was a marriage which almost did not happen. On his way to the church ceremony, he was ambushed along the road in Murchison Falls National Park by the notorious rebel Joseph Kony. Kony's reputation for murder and mayhem in Uganda during this period was legendary. Gilbert miraculously escaped and was married that same day of March 8, 1996, to his sweetheart bride.

As a young adult, G. was ordained to gospel ministry in 1997 and eventually was sent to start new churches and train pastors in the Paidha and Nebbi Districts, all the while working as a government teacher. He resigned his government position in 2008, moved to another district, and began teaching in a small Bible institute after finishing his Bible studies there.

We met G. in Kampala, Uganda, in 2019 at our classroom held on a privately owned property of a missionary associate. G. was always present in class twice each year and demonstrated a high-level understanding of both the subject matter and ministry intelligence. We had established a pattern over the years of taking notice of those pastors and church leaders who demonstrated a competency for ministry, a grasp of the theological content, and also a passion for training others. I knew that G. had been a teacher because we always had to know when the teacher's scheduled school breaks were so our classes could include them. It would not have made any sense for us to do otherwise. Long before he graduated G. had been teaching the GBTF material in his church and to other church leaders.

On many occasions over the last few years, we have noticed the raw determination G. demonstrates in getting to a class while

## WHY TRAIN THE NATIONALS?

adapting to various conditions. Last year during rainy season he took a bus to the teaching site, but the bus got mired in the mud, and he was forced to take a motorcycle the rest of the way. A few miles from his destination the motorbike got swamped, and G. was forced to walk the remaining few miles. He trudged on in his knee-length rubber boots and opened the class. Most Westerners would have waited for the dry season.

G. humbly says:

> As a national it is easy for us to reach certain areas which might be hard for a foreigner. When I go to some districts I sleep on the dusty floor of a grass thatched hut. There is no hotel one can use but as a national I can adjust to such a situation.

We have always known that nationals are better equipped for native ministry because of their knowing the local languages, but no one says it better than G. In our correspondence with him, he reminds us of the educational benefits of nationals working among their own people:

> As nationals, we speak more than one language and our trainers do as well. If there is anything hard to understand we can easily explain it to them. This makes the learning easy and interactive, and ultimately cost-effective.

G.'s statement also reminds us of the cost difference of supporting a Western couple or family doing ministry on a foreign field as opposed to training and equipping a national believer. Global Baptist Training Foundation can effectively train and assist fifty active pastors a month with the funding needed to support a Western missionary family over the same time. With over a hundred trainers presently training and holding classes each month, the exponential benefits of training the indigenous are rapidly expanding. G. adds:

> When national trainers train national trainees, real discipleship takes place because the trainer and the trainee speak the same tongue; they share the same culture and worldview; and they face similar challenges which allows for normal relatability and problem-solving.

The results of trained church leaders starting new churches who are reaching thousands of new believers has captivated both our organization and nationals themselves to think differently about everything. Consequently, national leaders across the continent are seeing themselves and their ministries in a new light.

Once again G. adds:

> The lessons are so inspiring to the trainers and the students that the classes continue to increase from country to country. After getting this theological learning you cannot remain the same. The pastors go from loving to study to needing to study because in Africa, it is difficult to get books and other quality written materials for ministry. GBTF has solved this by producing these detailed syllabi in many theological disciplines. GBTF is providing us a limitless future through well-trained personnel in our churches.

G., among many other GBTF-trained leaders, has caught the vision of 2 Tim 2:1–7 whereby the apostle Paul sets forth *how* we are to *move* and *multiply* the gospel forward. G. is one of many through whom the baton is being passed.

## PASTOR J. T.

> The training of our nationals is changing the spiritual landscape of Liberia and all of the African continent.

In 2016, J. contacted our office through the GBTF website and made application for classes to be held in Liberia. I met him in January of 2017 for the first time when he picked me up at the Monrovia airport for our initial classroom in Liberia. We held that first class with nearly sixty-five pastors gathered at the Baptist health center in an overcrowded building in the central town of Gbarnga, about two hours from the airport.

J. was born into a Christian family and was brought to faith in Christ at an early age. His family's early tribal origins were from a warrior class. Both his father and mother were committed believers and worked in an American mission organization based near their home village in the interior of the country. When he was three years old, he accidentally drank a small glass of acid left within arm's reach on a worktable. In the early sixties, there were no paved roads outside the village, and the closest hospital was thirty miles away. Somehow his parents reached the hospital before J. was overcome, and he survived. Although he was unable to swallow anything for several weeks, he lived on intravenous liquids until his throat was healed sufficiently to swallow solid food. Miraculously, he suffered no life-altering effects into adolescence.

Shortly after I first met him, he told me that one of the systemic problems in Liberia historically has been poverty. The second-greatest problem is education. The vast majority (85 percent) of Liberians are functionally illiterate. Add to that the continuous bouts of political corruption and dependence upon the United States for grants and foreign aid for decades, and the county has fallen way behind as an underdeveloped nation.

Because of his vast experience and maturity as a Christian leader, J. was elected as the field coordinator for regional Baptists and has held that position for several years. He laments the fact that most of the pastors who lead churches all over the country have had little formal education. Most of them have not had the opportunity to finish high school. He remembers that when American missionaries first came to the rural areas, many children were being taught by pictures and object lessons regularly. Unfortunately, the missionaries never began a system by which nationals were prepared theologically so they could deepen the work that had been started.

J. is definitely a survivor in many ways. In his early thirties, Liberia was thrust into the first of two civil wars which devastated the country. J. fled with his young family to Ghana where he lived over much of the fifteen years of conflict taking place in his home country. He had been in the ministry already for over eight years and decided that his ministry would now be to supply food and other needs for those who had fled into the bush country (jungle) to escape the wrath of the rebel leaders and their clans.

On one of those excursions, he was taken into custody by a rebel group outside of the capitol while he was traveling. He was placed in the back seat of a car with four rebel soldiers. He was sitting between two of them in the back seat headed to a death house. At a government road stop in the way, one of the few remaining, he was told to vacate the vehicle by a government-backed soldier. The soldier had no reason to do this other than it being an act of God. He didn't know J. personally and had no reason to make such a demand. His captors had no choice but to allow him to be taken out of the car. J. later said that had it not been for that soldier at that particular moment making that happen, he would have been killed within the hour.

Before knowing about J.'s warrior heritage, I remember on one occasion at the beginning of the Liberian rainy season, J. was taking us across Liberia to a remote area through several hours of jungle over unpassable roads when we got hopelessly stuck. It was nearing dark, and the opportunity to get out of there before nightfall was quickly passing. J. exited the vehicle, borrowed a machete from a fellow traveler in a similar condition and began to hack a path through the heavy brush on both sides of the road where our diesel-powered truck was sitting. Then he recruited five or six men to push us out of the rut in which we were stuck.

Within moments, we were free from the mud which had engulfed the vehicle up to the axles. In that moment, while hearing the grunts of the men pushing the vehicle, the commanding voice of leader J., and the incredible roar of the diesel engine, I realized I was in the presence of a different kind of man, and a warrior true to his tribal origins. J. is, and continues to be, a significant leader and trainer in the Liberian GBTF organization.

Just over five years later, in 2023, we graduated over one hundred pastors, deacons, evangelists, and several women from our theological coursework. They had completed fourteen courses of theological study. Incredibly, these nationals and those they in turn trained have launched over six hundred new church plants in West Africa alone.

J. says, "GBTF has revolutionized the Baptist church movement in Liberia."

Since that first class in 2017, with all the new churches dotting the Liberian landscape, they realize that it is still the spiritual morning in West Africa. Students are now planting churches in Guinea and Ghana, and soon classes will open in Togo, the Ivory Coast, Sierra Leone, and Guinea Bassau.

J. says:

> After many years of praying for an open door for nationals to get theological training, it has finally arrived through Global Baptist Training Foundation. Our pastors could never afford or have access to expensive Bible college or seminary training. Global Baptist Training Foundation is vitally changing the spiritual landscape of Liberia and all of the African continent.

## PASTOR D. N.

> Nationals who can learn theology where they live is a great blessing. This method of local classrooms allows all our pastors to gather and learn together not far from home and yet still be able to get the finest learning materials we have ever known. My vision for the future is to train more nationals who will then train others just like I have done.

Pastor D. was born in Burundi in 1981. His father, who had two wives, also fathered eleven other children in a highly dysfunctional home. His parents took the children to a local church, but the church would not allow the father to be a member because of his marital situation.

On Sunday mornings, D. would get up early so his father could take all the children to a village medicine man who gave them traditional concoctions rooted in animist worship. When they returned from the medicine man's house, they would go to the church's Sunday school. D. realized early in his life that he could not worship two different kinds of gods. His dad's sympathies were more with the medicine man's religious system, which included drinking large amounts of banana beer.

Finally, in 1999, when D. was seventeen years old, he gave his life over to Jesus Christ in church on Sunday morning. He went home and told his dad that he would no longer drink banana beer and take the traditional medicines from the village medicine man. His father warned him that without the protection of the medicines, spirits would overwhelm him and destroy his life. He would have no power over them and the world would become his enemy.

D. refused to go back to the old life and was baptized a few weeks later, saying, "I was a bad man, and my works merited eternal punishment. But, by God's grace, I became God's servant."

In 2004, at the age of twenty-two, D. stopped his secondary school education and decided to pursue a call to ministry. He immediately began to attend a Bible institute not far from where he lived. He finished his initial studies in 2008 and, because he was single, became a non-ordained pastor at the Gitega Baptist Church near where he had finished his Bible training. In September of that same year, he met and married his wife. She encouraged him to go back and finish his secondary school so he could ultimately attend the university to study marketing. D. was forced to leave her at home alone for several long months while he studied.

D. finished his marketing degree but finds his greatest fulfillment in using his GBTF training to train other nationals to reach the lost with the gospel and start new churches. Unlike all his other educational experiences, D'.s commitment to the GBTF curriculum is based on how the training is so easily passed on to other nationals without having to go to the larger cities. He commented:

> Nationals who can learn theology where they live is a great blessing. This method of local classrooms allows all our pastors to gather and learn together not far from home and yet still be able to get the finest learning materials we have ever known. My vision for the future is to train more nationals who will then train others just like I have done.

# CHAPTER FIVE

## What Has Happened?

DURING THE FIRST FEW years of the foundation's work of training indigenous pastors, I began to see that we were planting the seeds of a much greater harvest than we knew anything about at the time. The principles of 2 Tim 2:1–7 include the commitment of doctrinal training to leaders who will in turn commit that teaching to others. It is to be a continuous season of handing off the baton to other leaders who replicate and reproduce the same content of teaching in others. Class after class in one African nation after another allowed us to see a coming explosion of spiritual fruit on the horizon. Most of our trainers, once taught, begin training exercises in their home churches. Because many of them are in the bush or remote from the urban centers, the impact on both the trainer and the churches can be significant. One of our trainers commented:

> Through the training foundation, I have been equipped like never before with theological knowledge and the skills to serve God more effectively. The training has deeply influenced my ministry for serving with my local pastor and our church has benefitted in many ways.
> (See J. O. W.'s story at the end of this chapter.)

We know now that this impact on local churches has been significant because of the explosion of new church plants begun by many young men who are now in ministry. But now, over a decade of work later, another phenomenon is also coming to pass. Global Baptist Training Foundation has over two hundred trainers reproducing their own training in multiple classrooms in over twenty-five countries! While at one point, I personally held 8–10 classrooms per year, there are oftentimes that many classes a month. Two components have come together that we could not have imagined at the beginning of our journey.

The first is church planting. One day in 2016 the director of an organization which raises money for church planting called me and asked for a meeting. We met for lunch, and he asked me to consider his organization partnering with us to fund GBTF-trained men to start new church plants. The plan was to give $50 a month for one year to a trained man to help him launch a new church. After some prayer and counsel, we decided to move ahead on the offer. Including those churches started before this partnership began, GBTF has now had the privilege of launching over 1,600 new church plants in East, West, and South Africa through trained nationals.

To give you an idea of what trained indigenous men can accomplish, since January of 2017, over six hundred new church plants have been launched in Liberia alone. Several hundred more were launched from 2019–23 in East Africa after opening Uganda, Kenya, Ethiopia, Burundi, and Tanzania. In 2024 alone 455 new church plants were launched. One of our regional coordinators reported this:

> These new church plants launched by trained nationals are having an incredible impact on the natives of this whole area to the extent that other denominational churches who don't preach the gospel are embittered because large numbers of their people are fleeing their dead churches to hear the gospel of Jesus Christ.
> (See Pastor N.'s story at the end of this chapter.)

As I look back now, I had initially been so focused on the training aspect of the nationals that I had not fully considered church planting as it has developed with this new arm of GBTF. I'm glad

## WHAT HAS HAPPENED?

this myopia only lasted for a short time in our organization's development! God's plan is always much bigger than our own, but it still surprises me day after day to see the larger picture. Today, it's clear to see that the national pastors and others who go out to launch new church plants are highly motivated by their training and not the money. The evidence tells us that more church plants have now been launched by unsupported planters than supported. However, for some of the neediest pastors, the extra stipend puts some food on their family's tables and gas in their motor scooters for travel.

During this time, we have also developed a reporting system for all our church planters, the trainers who hold classrooms, and other national leaders, so they can report all their activity in quarterly reports. By the end of the fourth quarter of 2024, with the majority of these church plants reporting, over 50,000 individuals were reported to have come to faith in Christ in that one year alone, with over 45,000 of this total baptized and added to their respective churches. Others are taking baptism classes or awaiting the beginning of rainy season so that there is actually water for baptisms. After thirteen years of sowing the seed of training nationals, they are now beginning to multiply their own numbers exponentially. Pastor F. S. declared:

> Over the years, I have seen many groups come to teach our people. They come maybe once or twice, but that is all. They do not establish any permanent teaching strategy. GBTF is not like this. They have come year after year and completed their entire program with our group of pastors. At the completion of the final course our men wore GBTF graduation robes and received their diploma for completing their theological training. The impact of their training has resulted in church growth, scores of new churches started, and hundreds of new believers all over our country.

(See Pastor F. S.'s story at the end of this chapter.)

As this book is being written, the foundation is beginning to move into the northern cradle of Africa which, being predominantly Muslim, represents a completely different demographic than the rest of the continent. There will be significant challenges, unique methods required, and yet, a deep commitment to the same organic principles of 2 Tim 2:1–7. This scenario will be revisited throughout the Middle East and into the 10/40 window as well. As we continue to expand our footprint by training nationals it will be important to continually revisit the underlying purpose of the foundation in training and then empowering the indigenous. Notice training comes first! Empowerment comes through the learning process. Nationals everywhere I have personally taught instinctively know that knowledge is power. The "knowing" part of power is important. You cannot exercise power you don't know you possess. The second part of genuine power is the exercising of it in real time and in real terms. For many national Christians this has not been their privilege to experience.

For instance, I have been in many nations both in Africa and elsewhere where mission organizations owned their own property and buildings. Sometimes this is even true of church buildings and educational ministries. This is stifling to the national's spirit because they have no possession of the process or final results. The nationals may work in them and maintain them, but they don't actually own them. Their Western mentors own them and may actually control them financially. I have also witnessed Western missionaries charge other Western missionaries for the use of these properties to conduct ministries or operate hostels for visitors. This kind of missions philosophy deeply undermines and usurps the indigenous spirit. The nationals cannot fathom this kind of behavior. They would never use ministry ownership of property or buildings to "lord it over" other believers or leaders. It is repugnant to them because they cannot imagine Christ utilizing kingdom resources in this manner.

On top of the nationals taking great pride and joy in owning the fruits of their labor in Christ, there is great joy in the numbers of graduations and new students being produced by the nationals themselves. In February of 2025, I attended the graduation ceremonies of groups in Western Rwanda and Burundi, equaling over two hundred graduates from the theological training program.

Here is the amazing fact about these particular graduations. I did not personally teach one of the entire twenty-eight classes held in both countries! *Trained national trainers taught every class!*

In Western Rwanda alone, after the 2025 graduation, there were over seven hundred students waiting for their first class to begin! Even the national leaders were surprised at the sheer number of believers who were waiting to take classes. They had never seen anything like this with other mission agencies with whom they had any association. One of our key trainers commented:

> There were several Western organizations and individuals who appeared to us to be trying to build their own little empires in Africa, but I now see trained nationals are actually building the kingdom of God. There is just no real comparison.
> (See F. S.'s story at the end of this chapter.)

Over the last few years, I have had to ask myself the question from where this desire for learning and education had come. Was it a sudden phenomenon or had it really been there all along? The fact remains that Western missionaries had been in the country for nearly a hundred years. Why had this passion for theological training not already been tapped by earlier evangelical missionaries? I cannot answer that question.

The second component we didn't anticipate happened in 2021. We were introduced to an organization whose sole mission is to build buildings for congregations in developing nations reaching one hundred or more members without sufficient resources to build on their own. I met with the director of the organization and submitted our first request for a building in one of our African countries where an evangelical church had not been known to exist for generations. They took on the project, and that building was raised despite much pagan opposition. It now stands as a visible monument to God's glory in that place where no memory of an evangelical church existed!

One of the most poignant memories of the last few years was a church building we had the privilege to build for a rapidly growing village church in the heart of Uganda. The building was financed by one of our partners, and it is by far the largest church building in the area, seating up to 750 people. Many of the people who watched it going up day after day *knew* that it was being built out of local materials but that it would ultimately be *owned* by the Americans who financed it. When the building was finished the city council, the police, the local military, and other dignitaries from all over Uganda came to the service of over three thousand people inside and outside the new structure. I was asked to participate in the actual dedication ceremony (one of many that day), and I read the bronze plaque cemented into the cornerstone. After reading the plaque I had the joy of telling those hundreds of people gathered that day in that little unknown village that the lowly members of this new church were also now the sole owners of this new building. It was completely and entirely their church! Words are simply not capable of describing the joy of what ownership meant to them on that dedication day.

Because we have two such organizations who have partnered with us for erecting buildings where they are needed, our long-term plan is to build at least one church building in all fifty-four African countries where Global Baptist Training Foundation classes can be held. In larger countries like the Democratic Republic of Congo, several will be built regionally so men and women can reach the church teaching site without excessive travel. In many of our classes, individuals will travel up to 10–12 hours by bus, motorcycle, and on foot to reach a classroom location.

During our training classes in Liberia, we scheduled classes during the height of the rainy season in 2018–20. The stories we heard of pastors struggling to get to the training site were in many cases heroic. They would show up late on Monday when class had already started, tired, hungry, soaked, and yet excited to be there for the class. We would embrace them, love them, and get them caught up for the remaining days of class. I would go to my room each evening weary from teaching but energized by their example of selflessness and commitment to what was really important.

## WHAT HAS HAPPENED?

Our hope is that by strategically locating buildings for new church plants much of this painful and costly travel can be greatly reduced or in some cases eliminated for many students.

One of the most profound and surprising things about the foundation's success in training nationals over this thirteen-year period are the amazing human beings we have encountered. African people are, without doubt, the most gracious, giving, and generous people we have met anywhere in the world. Whether it's in a government office, a city restaurant, or a jungle village home, Africans all over the continent are committed to improving life for themselves and others around them. There is much to learn from their selfless examples.

My greatest teaching moments have happened in these very classrooms throughout the continent where I see men and women desiring to gain biblical knowledge and training where they live, which they in turn can leverage for the kingdom of God. The passion for training is indicative of a long-standing vacuum being filled. One of our trainers noted:

> The fact that Africa has so many pastors and leaders who have never had any theological training demonstrates this system of on-site teaching is exactly what we needed here.
> (See J. M.'s story at the end of this chapter.)

We couldn't simply agree more! I have had several people ask me if we could do the same thing online or through Zoom classes periodically. The answer is both yes and no. A few months ago, I held a Zoom class for a group of pastors in Bangladesh. We also conduct some official meetings this way throughout the calendar year. However, in the end, the reality is that you cannot have *impact* without *contact*. There is something that happens in a face-to-face classroom experience that cannot happen on Zoom. Remember, Socrates made this dictum the essence of his teaching method! The technology is also a deterrent to online training. Many of the pastors we train are from villages and towns that have nothing but spotty electricity. The resources for internet, computers, etc., are just not available to the majority of those we train. That being said, we make it our policy to provide every church planter and trainer a smartphone so they are able to take good pictures of their work and can communicate to fellow laborers in their larger area. They are also trained to use the GBTF app on their phone to log their class results, church plant evangelism results, etc. This has proven to be a complete game changer for enabling the continental team to know each other and interact as necessary.

Since 2012, we have witnessed the indigenous leaders faithfully leveraging their training: nationals training nationals, trained nationals starting hundreds of churches, and nationals reaching their own people for Christ by the tens of thousands for the glory of God.

So what is the plan for the next decade? After developing a presence in all fifty-four African countries Global Baptist Training Foundation is focused on continuing the trek up into the Middle East and on into the 10/40 window nations where approximately 3.4 billion live having never heard the gospel of Jesus Christ. Incredibly, just over 3.5 percent of all missionaries are willing to go there. This means that it is imperative that nationals be trained to reach their own populations in this strategic region. We are praying that we will be poised and prepared to train and send them forth into the harvest.

May God give us his great grace to fulfill his mission to the world. We constantly remind ourselves that GBTF is only one story in God's far bigger story. There are countless opportunities in which we all can engage now in the work of empowering nationals to reach their nations. Much of the 10/40 window of nations and peoples remain in desperate need of the gospel. Only the Lord of the harvest can lead us in this enormous effort in making Christ known globally. However, it will require a strategy, or perhaps many strategies by many churches and church mission outreaches. One of the most invigorating things in the world is to see how God calls each of us to serve in some unique way. This much we know: God uses the theological training of the nationals powerfully and pervasively! Because they are the masters of their languages, dialects, and culture, they must be prepared to lead the way in reaching their nations with the gospel. I believe we are on the cusp of a harvest of souls unlike our world has ever seen since the days of the apostles.

First, we must see what is in front of us. As Jesus told us, "*Look* unto the fields for they are white and ready for harvest" (John 4:35; emphasis added). The time for hesitation is through. Now it is time to act. So what is our next step? Pray! Jesus said, "*Pray* to the Lord of the harvest that He will send forth laborers into the harvest" (Matt 9:38; emphasis added).

Get your church missions team praying about how to change the missions culture of your church to make the training of nationals central to everything else you do. Once that becomes your focus your actions will take on greater meaning and purpose.

Allow me to humbly ask another question. What is your mission plan in reaching your world? If you haven't already considered making some changes in your church's foreign outreach strategy, why not now? The best place to begin that process is right in your own church community. If training nationals to reach their nations with the gospel has not been a key focus until now, endeavor to make it one! Pray about an area of the globe that can become your focus for advancing the gospel. That area of interest may very well be a part of the globe that *has been* previously reached with the gospel and has groups of believers with whom you could work. Remember nationals want and need training that they have access to and can immediately utilize. Once they have received the kind of training that doctrinally grounds them in the word of God and instructs them on how to preach and teach it, they become powerful ambassadors for the kingdom. We have seen living proof of this for well over a decade now. If I were a lawyer, I believe I can rightly say that there is indisputable proof!

Finally, pray that God would show you some inroads to the place of his choice at this very time for your church. God is working mightily in the Middle East today. Despite the lack of real news emerging from the region, there are multitudes of Muslim and Jewish people open to the gospel today which was not possible twenty years ago. There are numbers of common people in Islamic countries like Iran who are being exposed to the gospel and fleeing their former religion. Then there is East Asia in the 10/40 window that continues to ripen for a future harvest of souls. Reaching nationals with the gospel or identifying nationals who have come to faith in Christ is the first step in training and empowerment to reach others. Remember, God's plan is perfect, so don't think that you or the missions team at your church needs to have all the answers. It is truly a journey of taking the first step, and then watching God show you the path for a real missions adventure.

## PASTOR N. R. A.

> In my opinion, Western missionaries have had a limited impact on the churches they start in Africa because once they leave, it is a serious challenge for national pastors to maintain the churches started by Western missionaries.

Pastor N. was born March 31, 1974, in Mbarara, Western Uganda. His parents, at the time, were members of the local Anglican church, and so N. was baptized by the Anglican priest as an infant and also confirmed by him at twelve years of age. At confirmation, the priest laid his hands on his head, affirming him as a true Christian and member of the church. N. said:

> I grew up full of pride, believing that Anglicanism was the only true way to heaven. It wasn't until I turned twenty years of age that I heard the gospel as spoken in the word of God.

On September 11, 1994, N. repented of his sin and trusted Jesus Christ personally as his Savior from sin, something he never knew was required of him before. He said from that day forward he had great joy serving the Lord as one of God's children. Shortly after his salvation, Naboth began studying to become a lawyer at the local university, but he could never escape the inner desire he had to serve the Lord with his entire life. One day while walking to a service with a local missionary woman she encouraged him to begin taking classes at the Bible institute her husband had begun.

# WHAT HAS HAPPENED?

While finishing his classes at the institute, N. met and married his wife, who was a faithful Christian from N.'s area. They were blessed with four children: three boys and one girl. All of the children are now faithfully serving the Lord in their own respective churches and raising families of their own.

In 2018, while meeting with three other pastors, the entire group decided to start a fellowship of like-minded churches from all over East Africa. Little did anyone know that just a year later the leadership of Global Baptist Training Foundation would be asked to speak at their very fellowship meeting in the same town of Mbarara. It was there I would meet N., who was the president of the new fellowship. The gathered pastors sat and listened as I laid out the strategy we had taken to train pastors all over the African continent.

Just three months later we opened our first classroom among the Ugandans in Kampala about five hours north. It was well attended, and, for three years, my ministry partners and I returned twice each year to teach all of the fourteen classes in our curriculum. During this time of training these pastors, we had the opportunity of starting over 115 new churches among them and seeing hundreds of new believers added to these new church plants. In Mbarara we had the privilege of helping Pastor N. raise a new building that seats over 750 people and now serves as a key training center for GBTF in Uganda. Since 2023 GBTF has opened five training centers, four in Uganda and one in South Sudan. The South Sudan center is the first GBTF church plant in that war-ravaged country.

N declared:

> These new church plants launched by trained nationals are having an incredible impact on the natives of this whole area to the extent that other denominational churches who don't preach the gospel are embittered because large numbers of their people are fleeing their churches to hear the gospel of Jesus Christ.

## PASTOR S. F.

> While some Western organizations seem to be laboring to build their own empires, trained nationals are using their educational and ministry resources to build the kingdom of God. There is simply no comparison between these two models.

F. was born in the Fizi Southern Kiva District of the Democratic Republic of Congo in 1977. He was the seventh of twelve children whose father kept cattle for a living. He was taught to work hard and learned early the disciplines of rural life. His parents were believers, but F. did not come to know Jesus Christ as Savior until the age of twenty.

In November of 1997, he had been invited to an all-night prayer meeting by a lady named Diana, a friend of the family. Early in the evening the pastor invited to the event brought a message to the group about the love of God. F. said:

> I was so touched by the word of God realizing how much God loved me in order for Christ to die for my sin, I wanted to know him and trust him as my Savior. It was that very evening I became a believer in Jesus Christ.

Just a year later in 1998, civil war broke out in the DRC. By August, rebels had taken over the area where F. lived, and he was arrested by a group of Congolese soldiers who immediately imprisoned him. He was to be killed the following day. On the same day of F.'s planned execution, a frontline soldier had been brought to the area who had been severely injured and needed blood. All of the prisoners were checked for blood type to donate blood but none of them matched the injured soldier. Finally, the doctor yelled aloud, "Is there no one who can help this soldier live?" F. blurted out that he would give his blood if it matched, and, to everyone's surprise, it was an exact match. Not only was the soldier saved that day but F.'s gift of blood bought him his own freedom. When F. was asked about the incident he simply replied, "To God be all the glory, because today I am serving Him."

## WHAT HAS HAPPENED?

I first met F. in 2013. He had become the pastor of the host church where we had begun to train pastors in Kigali, Rwanda. F. was in his early thirties and had been asked to pastor the church on the compound of a significant group of Baptist churches in the capitol city. Although it was an influential church, it paid poorly, and each year when I would return, I couldn't help but notice that F. seemed to be filling a post that he would one day outlive in terms of his potential for a larger sphere of leadership. I encouraged him to remain faithful and open to the Lord's leadership in his life. One day in October 2018, before I started my ninth class with the Rwandan students, F. informed me he had decided to resign his church. I asked him why and he simply replied, "I want to become a national trainer with GBTF." I nearly fell out of my chair.

Since that day in 2018, F. has become the head of the spear for GBTF in Africa. He is now our GBTF director for all of Africa and will open six new countries a year until 2032 when we hope to be engaged in all fifty-four African member states. F. has seen many Western missionaries and agencies come and go over the last twenty-five years and believes that there are several reasons why Global Baptist Training Foundation is growing so rapidly on the African continent.

He commented:

> Over the years, I have seen many groups come to teach our people. They come maybe once or twice, but that is all. They do not establish any permanent teaching strategy. GBTF is not like this. They have come year after year and completed their entire program with our group of pastors. At the completion of the final course our men wore GBTF graduation robes and received their diplomas for completing their theological training. The impact of their training has resulted in church growth, scores of new churches started, and hundreds of new believers all over Rwanda.

F. added:

> While some Western organizations seem to be laboring to build their own empires, trained nationals are using

their educational and ministry resources to build the kingdom of God. There is simply no comparison between these two models.

(Let me quickly add something here. We, here at the foundation, know that we are not the only group working to enable greater ministry among the thousands of nationals all over Africa. We are simply wanting our readers to recognize how greatly God has blessed his work throughout Africa being done by Africans empowered through their own theological training. It is nothing short of amazing to see God's plan in 2 Tim 2:1–7 actually producing this kind of exponential multiplication.)

It is our hope that many more churches and church leaders will adopt a plan which encourages the training of national church leaders all over the globe where they presently exist. As the focus to reach the 10/40 window nations continues, our prayer is that God would provide the critical contacts for developing redemptive relationships, discipleship, and classrooms preparing those coming to faith in Christ for the training of others.

## PASTOR J. M.

> The fact that Africa has so many pastors and leaders who have never had any theological training demonstrates this system of on-site teaching is exactly what we needed here.

Pastor J. has been a lifelong resident in the country of Kenya and is now one of the elder trainers among the GBTF community in his native country. Born in 1956, J. was twelve years old when he became a Christian in 1968. He was in his family's church on a Saturday evening while his pastor was preaching a message from the book of Jonah. Hearing that God had called the city of Nineveh to repentance from their sin, he sensed the gravity of his own waywardness from God. That Saturday night was the night he turned from darkness to light through the gospel of Jesus Christ. Not long after he was converted to Christ, he fell into a sharp disagreement with his father and left home emotionally scarred and bearing a deep grievance against him.

He said:

> I left home thinking that I would either go and commit suicide or that I would never return home again. But God brought me to a pastor whom God used to change my entire outlook on my life, and I returned home a few months later. Not long after, I surrendered to God for ministry and immediately enrolled in a Bible college for pastoral training. Little did I know that my previous affliction would result in God calling me to serve Him!

Not long after J. started his classes, he met his future wife and God blessed him with seven children who are all Christians and serving God in their local churches.

When Global Baptist Training Foundation came to Kenya he recognized how swiftly and efficiently the training was provided to them module by module and course by course.

Pastor J. stated:

> The fact that Africa has so many pastors and leaders who have never had any theological training or access to it demonstrates this system of on-site teaching is exactly what we needed here.

As we came to understand the personal benefits of training for nationals, we began to understand the national's mindset about leveraging their training for doing ministry. I noticed that during their training there were particular courses which excited them more than others. One of those was a course on evangelism and church planting. We started getting reports after teaching that course that the pastors were going back to their churches and teaching what they had learned. The impact was noticeable. Within months, many new church plants were launched by former deacons, evangelists, and young men who had committed to ministry and had been ordained by their churches to go out and start church plants. These pastors were trained through GBTF. Consequently, one of our great emphases has become church planting support and assisting those trained men who wanted to launch new congregations, especially in the rural areas.

The vision for these church plants is to build buildings in strategic areas where hundreds of pastors can come to receive the training they need for their ministries. GBTF now has church building partners, and this model is presently being practiced in many countries. Many East African countries will soon see their own churches built for both evangelism and the training of trainers for Christ.

## PASTOR J. O. W.

> This story is not just about my transformation but what God can do when we all surrender our lives to his purpose. I am passionate about the work of nationals training nationals through our new church plants which also serve as training centers where we can provide continuous theological education.

Pastor J. was born in the Kigoma Region of Western Tanzania in 1967. Eleven years later in 1978, he recalled a gospel event in his village that resulted in his coming to faith in Christ along with several others in his community. He joined the choir and participated in evangelistic campaigns yearly, growing deep in his love for the Lord and various ministry opportunities. He was also a good student in school, and this opened several educational doors including learning mechanical engineering in Northern Tanzania where he finished college.

In 1994, he moved to Dar Es Salaam to work, all the while continuing to labor for the Lord in his local church where he got involved in publishing Christian literature used for evangelism. During this early period of his career, he met and married his wife. They have been blessed with a family of seven children who all have come to faith in Christ and serve in their local church. Over the last decade, Pastor J. lost all of his siblings in a tragic accident, and he personally took responsibility for the care of twenty of his extended family members into his own household. He says it has been a huge challenge, but God has blessed him greatly for his sacrifice. Many of them are musical, and they, in turn, have used their talents in their local church to bless many others.

After receiving an invitation from a group of pastors in Tanzania, Pastor J. attended our GBTF classes in the capitol city and then graduated in 2023. Like many other local leaders, Pastor J. said:

> Through the training foundation, I have been equipped like never before with theological knowledge and the skills to serve God more effectively. The training has deeply influenced my ministry for serving with my local pastor and our church has greatly benefitted.

Because of the life difficulties Pastor J. has faced, his training has allowed him to come alongside many other individuals who have faced similar tragedy and hardship in their lives. It has become an essential part of his work for the Lord. His prayer is that his journey in Christ will inspire many others to live with purpose and a heart for serving others in their own Christian journeys.

Thinking back, Pastor J. said:

> Actually, this story is not just about my transformation but what God can do when we all surrender our lives to his purpose. I am truly passionate about the work of nationals training other nationals through our new church plants which also serve as training centers where we can provide continuous theological education.

# CHAPTER SIX

## Protocols for Change

WHEN THE LORD BEGAN to lead me into the present ministry of training nationals for Christian service in their own countries, I could never have understood the magnitude of what He had planned. Had I known that, it likely would have shocked my senses. I say that not because the work is necessarily overwhelming but rather that the results have been overwhelming. I have come to realize two things about making these kinds of decisions in ministry life. First, it's not all about me and what I do or have done. It's about God and all He wants to do through earthen vessels like us.

Second, ministry success is not about one's background, education, spiritual gifts, abilities, ego, self-driven ambition, or any other possible human contribution. It is all about one's simple willingness to obey God, submission to his plan, and faithfulness to his call each day you get out of bed. Every day I face a new sunrise I have learned to simply and humbly cry out, "God, you are in charge; I'm not." It will be no different with you as an individual Christian, pastor, teacher, missions director, etc.

I believe change in this matter of missions among tens of thousands of Bible-believing evangelical churches is going to require the same response. We must change the missions paradigm in our churches if we are going to move and multiply the gospel all around the world. I can promise you that it will be necessary in the 10/40 window. We simply cannot adopt a pioneer method of sending missionary couples who don't know the nuance of native languages, the navigational demands of a host culture, or the naivety of thinking they can love the people like those who have lived among them all their lives. We must begin to recognize that the return on the investment of our mission dollars demands we begin looking to the nationals to help solve the problem of world evangelization. The time for training nationals to reach their nations is now, and we must begin to think as clearly as Paul thought about world evangelization in 2 Tim 2.

I want to provide some simple steps for how every church can begin to implement changes in missions policies and programs. These ideas are not novel or new, but I hope they will offer some fresh reminders on how to move forward with a clear approach in the local church.

First, we need to:

## Cast a New Vision for a New and Refreshed Mission Policy

Oh yes, I know this one is tough. You will likely hear something like, "But pastor, we ain't never done it that way before!" It's true, change isn't easy for anyone. However, are you willing to leave things as they are and stand before Jesus and tell him why you left things as they are? Can you expect to hear him say, "Well done, thou good and faithful servant?"

Casting a vision means that you and the church recognize the singular importance of Paul's final words to Timothy just before he died for Christ. The training of indigenous pastors cannot remain an option but a mandate if you intend on casting a vision that truly impacts and enlarges your church's worldwide mission vision.

Secondly:

## Assess Where Your Church Is Now

This means that we must go line by line through our missions budgets and philosophy and consider making hard decisions about what is producing evangelism and church planting results and what is not. I know this first step is going to be the hardest step of all because you may very well have good and godly people who have committed themselves to a church mission or some other good work who you will have to consider either letting go on your budget or setting requirements for them to change themselves. Perhaps it can be as simple as reading the last two years of their monthly or bimonthly letters to know if the return on investment justifies their support. Stay with me. In the last ten years in training nationals, we have seen over 1,700 churches started by trained nationals as of this date with quarterly reports of theologically trained national-pastor-run church plants producing in excess of 25,000 to 30,000 converts to Christ each quarter. That is the average number per quarter this year of 2025. It will increase next year as we add an average of three hundred more church plants in Africa alone.

Culling your missionary expenditures is going to require you to truly commit to the process. A wonderful pastor friend of mine just recently did this and found that several of his missionaries inherited from a previous pastor were doing little more than collecting their support, saving for retirement, and accomplishing astonishing little in terms of their $6,800-a-month support invested by over sixty churches. This process of examining mission letters will not be easy or conclude in unanimous opinions. This means that it will require the collective efforts of every person on the missions committee because when all missions personnel see the same information, it will be easier to make the hard decisions as a body of concerned and committed believers.

Thirdly:

### Discover If Your Prospective Missionaries Truly Embrace the Importance of Empowering Nationals to Reach Their Own Nations with the Gospel

We have conducted hundreds of interviews with national pastors over the last fourteen years, and in nearly all of these interviews we are told the same thing by the indigenous leaders: "We want theological training more than we want your resources or your money."

## PROTOCOLS FOR CHANGE

This is a key part of process of whether or not to support a missionary candidate who wants your church to support their cause!

As we discovered earlier, nationals want training because they know that they can leverage that training for the kingdom of God for an entire lifetime of Christian service. On the other hand they also are keenly aware that money and resources are temporal and can be replaced as God provides. If there is a one key area in which we have failed in our missions efforts on a global scale, it is in this vital area of training. For whatever reason, many American and European missionaries have not made this the core focus of their own mission for the past 150 years.

Consider how central this point was in Paul's ultimate commission to Timothy in his final months on this earth. He commanded him no differently than Jesus did the first disciples on Mount Olivet. With clear imperatives he required Timothy to train the national leaders to train others, who would in turn train others both theologically (doctrinally) and generationally (continuously). I now understand these words better than I ever have in fifty years of ministry. Why? Because the results are frankly undeniable. In fact, by the time you read this book, the statistical results of GBTF of 2025 will be old news.

In short, we must demand the same from every missionary we support! We must ask them the hard questions regarding their sense of responsibility to train nationals to independently train their own target audiences.

Here is a good starter list when interviewing your missionary candidates:

1. What is the missionary mindset concerning being a pioneer or perpetuating training among existing believers?
2. How does the missionary view 2 Tim 2:1–7 in light of their mission?
3. Is the missionary theologically trained to capably train others? (We know that this is the ideal nationals desire.)

4. Does the missionary have an intentional plan? (Plans can be changed but modification assumes a plan is in place which can be modified!)
5. Will he travel back and forth to the field or does he plan on permanently settling? (Remember that settling on the field is extremely costly and therefore must be justified with a reasonable expectation of ROI.)
6. Has he established meaningful contacts on the field that give him a foothold from which to operate (translators, etc.)?
7. What is his exit strategy once his objective is accomplished? (This is important to hear because this means there is an end result which requires one!)

That means every prospective missionary must have better training for teaching and equipping nationals themselves. We have always said, "You cannot teach what you don't know." Therefore we must invest in sending mission couples/teams who are both well trained theologically but also have a clear vision for propagating the training among their national audiences. This will also change the way they look at their own tasks. Language school may very well become an obsolete requirement if there are English-speaking Christian nationals present who can become translators on the mission team. This bridges the communication and culture gap immediately for mission personnel in such environments. English is the language of choice in many places where the gospel is desperately needed. Finding translators is no longer a significant issue when this model is adopted. We have been successfully doing this for nearly fourteen years in Africa, East Asia, and South America. Translation has essentially become a nonissue!

This could also mean that mission personnel would not be required to be constantly present on any field when training sessions are not scheduled. We have found in nearly every developing country that poor students cannot afford to have class any more than two to three weeks a year because they must find ways to support their families the majority of the time. Within 2–3 years, depending on the particular situation, students can complete the fifteen courses we offer without any problem. Missionaries would then be free to move around and train in several locations or return home and work at preparing teaching materials, hold Zoom meetings, and communicate constantly on WhatsApp and the internet. In other words, mission couples or teams can be short-term yet carry on continuous ministry under certain conditions. This completely changes the missions paradigm and also changes the financial demands of support if short-term options work effectively. For years, I supported my family while teaching online while I was traveling. It was difficult at the time because internet was not dependable. Today, with the proliferation of 5G satellites, many Christians have the liberty to work from home or a distant location while doing many other tasks. This certainly opens the door for committed Christians to do just the same while teaching, training, and impacting national believers to reach their nations for Christ.

However, let's be honest. Even if our mission personnel decide to live on the field, the exponential results of their training in church planting and evangelism among the nationals will be well worth the investment! Churches would then be free to focus their missions dollars in certain areas of God's specific directives rather than trying to spread their resources among many. No one church can do it all, but thousands of churches can have an inestimable and eternal impact for Christ when we invest our missions dollars strategically under the leadership of the Holy Spirit.

Finally:

## Does Your Church See that Training Nationals Is the Missions Bulls-Eye?

We oftentimes underestimate the ability of God's people who populate our churches in grasping the big ideas behind our biblical mandates. What I mean is that we think we really can't get them as motivated as we leaders are about evangelism and church planting worldwide. This is a fallacy and a lie. I keenly remember the early days of our training organization when I thought I was the only one who "got it" in terms of what the Lord was calling us to do.

But everywhere I went and explained the mission in person I was always amazed at how many people came up to me and said stuff like, "Wow, this concept of training nationals makes perfect sense, why haven't we been doing this?"

So what are we to aim at in training national believers? Paul aimed at three clear prerequisites:

1. The record of the book of Acts and the Epistles tell the story.

In each city across Asia Paul and Barnabas appointed *faithful elders* for them in every church and town for the express purpose of church leadership (Acts 14:2–3; Titus 1:5). The description of potential elders as faithful reminds us that character lies at the core of the entire series of imperatives in this passage. The character of potential leaders is mentioned in light of the fact that in the previous chapter, all in Asia had forsaken the mission. Paul makes no compromise for those who had failed by lowering the bar. He maintains the absolute standard of faithfulness rooted in obedience. Only men of proven character can be trusted long-term with leadership in Christ-honoring churches. In the Eastern Bloc, including China, house church pastors are usually chosen on the basis of having suffered persecution, threats of death, and prison.

2. Local elders live in and understand how to navigate the culture.

It was not even considered that nonlocal pastors would be shipped in to lead culturally unique congregations. This makes perfect sense in terms of the comfort level of someone who might be hearing the gospel for the first time or of new believers. A local person was someone who could be trusted far easier because they looked and talked like them versus a foreigner who did represent their own cultural values. The apostles did not pastor the churches they started but trained leaders among them from that culture to lead the flocks. Far too often our missionaries start a church on location and then remain as pastor. This is not consistent with the NT pattern, nor is it effective long-term. It usually never results in a truly healthy church, nor does it allow the church to thrive in the

## PROTOCOLS FOR CHANGE

existing culture as it would if there were a locally trained leader among them.

I wish I had clearly understood this early in my career when I was planting churches in a unique culture not my own. Someone might say, "Well Timothy was not from Ephesus, so how could he successfully pastor that church?" I would answer that objection/question by simply pointing out that Timothy had been universally accepted as a member of Paul's team for some time. He had traveled extensively with the apostle and taken responsibilities to serve churches and the mission team, not to mention Paul, for several years. He had been deliberately circumcised at Paul's behest in order to further his acceptance among Greek audiences, had a Greek father, and spoke Greek and Hebrew fluently. Furthermore, Ephesus was a major Hellenistic city which had a large Greek-speaking population. It was a melting pot of Mediterranean culture and pagan religion which Timothy had interfaced with for much of his life and ministry. There would have been little that would have been foreign to him either culturally or personally. Therefore his acceptance and usefulness there would have offered little if any substantive barrier.

3. Local pastors speak the native tongue/dialect.

Speaking the native language well is an essential part of communicating the gospel. Nobody can duplicate the nuance of a local dialect or use the local colloquialisms better than the natives who live there. Nationals are able to present the gospel fluently and readily wherever the might be, and this is always a tremendous advantage for the advance of the gospel. When local, trained, and culturally knowledgeable nationals are present, the results move from addition to multiplication!

My prayer for you as a pastor or Christian leader would be to deeply consider what we have discussed throughout these pages. Without some real and objective thinking about what it means to train the indigenous believers around the world to multiply themselves through church planting and evangelism, the task is simply too great for outsiders to think otherwise. Paul's plan for Timothy was simple and straightforward, yet it is capable of transforming your missions program and instilling a revolutionary missionary spirit in your church. As we prepare to enter our fifteenth year of training nationals worldwide, we pray you will join with us in the exponential multiplication of training nationals to train nationals!

# Epilogue

DEPENDANCE ON THE REMNANTS of Western colonialism is a crutch. Training nationals is the most powerful method in fulfilling the Great Commission of Christ. When pastors and church leaders are trained and provided with sound biblical teaching with the ability to use ministry tools according to 2 Tim 2:1-7, then the gospel can be preached everywhere with ease. Trained national pastors can reach their communities more effectively because they already know the culture and language. Nationals can then train other nationals so the gospel multiplies exponentially. This indigenous principle must be obeyed and multiplied if we are to fulfill world evangelization.

Pastor N. R.

# Conclusion

SOME INCREDIBLY IMPORTANT VOICES need to be heard in our Christian experience. For instance, we need to daily hear God's voice from the authoritative Scriptures. We need to hear our pastors expound God's Word publicly in worship. We also need to hear our own Biblically informed consciences remind us daily of what is right and wrong. These voices are necessary to forming a worldview that makes our own voices worth being heard as God's image-bearers. But this volume reminds us that there are other voices among us in our Christian world that not only need to be heard but deserve to be heard; national believers.

I'm reminded of a story I read of an advertised woman's meeting where a well-known (and well paid) woman speaker known for her loud voice had been hired to address about 60 women and a handful of men. During a special session, however, instead of focusing on the women she had been hired to address, the special speaker gave the allotted speaking time to the handful of men present. Sadly, by the time this was pointed out to her the meeting time had officially run out.

Those of us in Christian ministry from the West also have very loud voices. Perhaps our voices are louder because of our training, resources, or cultural presence. But we must be careful not to measure our importance by the power we wield alone. In the mission endeavor before us there are no big Is and little yous. There is only the mission itself.

In AD 67 while Paul was languishing in his last imprisonment before his martyrdom, he gave Timothy his marching orders for all time in how to accomplish the mission of spreading the gospel. He had practiced these methods throughout his mission journeys and proven their efficacy in Galatia, Macedonia, Asia, and even on the little island of Crete. What we have discovered over the last 13 years about the empowerment of nationals through training has forced us to reassess not only how we think about missions but how we do missions. It is my hope and prayer that our discovery might become yours in recognizing why training the indigenous works!

# Bibliography

MacMullen, Ramsay. *Christianizing the Roman Empire: (A.D. 100-400)*. New Haven, CT: Yale University Press, 1984.
National Association of Evangelicals. "Statement of Faith." https://www.nae.org/statement-of-faith/.
Polhill, John B. *Acts*. Vol. 26 of *New American Commentary*. Nashville: Broadman, 1992.
Snavely, Bruce. *Indigenous: Missions Aimed at Training Nationals Globally*. Eugene, OR: Wipf & Stock, 2019.
Yohannan, K. P. *Come, Let's Reach the World*. Carrollton, TX: GFA, 2004.

www.ingramcontent.com/pod-product-compliance
Lightning Source LLC
Chambersburg PA
CBHW050838160426
43192CB00011B/2075